熟语大大字

Learn Chinese The Fun Way

汪惠迪　辑

谢世顺　译

梁锦泉
黄志强　插图
林德生

联邦出版社·联合早报

© 1994联邦出版（新）私人有限公司
A member of the Times Publishing Group
Times Centre
1 New Industrial Road
Singapore 1953

1994年初版

版权所有，不准以任何方式，
在世界任何地区，以中文或任何文字，
作全部或局部之翻印、仿制或转载。

ISBN 981 01 3046 5

Printed by B & Jo Enterprise Pte Ltd, Singapore

目 录

成语

俗语

惯用语

不胫而走 bù jìng ér zǒu

　　胫：小腿；走：跑。没有腿而跑得很快，比喻事物用不着宣传、推行，就很快地传播、流行开来。例如：中共中央政治局扩大会议上星期召开的消息以及江泽民传达的邓小平讲话精神，近日来在北京不胫而走。知识分子、青年学生和多数党政机关干部，从各种渠道听到有关消息后，普遍感到鼓舞。（《邓小平重新确立改革路线》，1992年2月21日《联合早报》第18版）

　　也说成"无胫而至（到达）"、"无胫而行（走）"或"不胫而驰（chí，快跑）"。

News Travels Fast

"Jing" means shin. This Chinese idiom means something travels very fast even without any shin. It is used to describe a piece of news which spreads rapidly without any effort to propagate it.

Example: "News about the expanded meeting of the Chinese Communist party Central Polibureau and message of Deng Xiaoping conveyed by Jiang Zemin travelled fast. Many people who heard the news from various sources were greatly encouraged." (Lianhe Zaobao 21/2/92)

不遗余力 bù yí yú lì

遗：留下；余力：没有用完的力量。一点儿也没有保留地用出全部力量。例如：有记者问建省（海南省）四年来当局"扫黄"的统计资料，邓鸿勋强调，嫖娼行为不符合社会主义经济特区准则，所以公安部门扫黄不遗余力，建省以来一共逮捕妓女400名，都送去再教育，辅导她们走向新生。（《洋浦不会成为"第二个上海租界"》，1992年3月28日《联合早报》第16版）

"遗"也说"留"。

Without Sparing Any Effort

This Chinese idiom literally reads as without reserving any strength.

Example: "On anti-vice operation in Hainan, Mr Deng Hongxun told reporters that for the last four years since Hainan became a province, the authorities had 'spared no effort' in the operation. A total of four hundred prostitutes had been rounded up and sent for re-education and rehabilitation." (Lianhe Zaobao 28/3/92)

茶余饭后 chá yú fàn hòu

茶：喝茶；饭：吃饭。指喝茶吃饭之后的一段空闲休息时间。现多用来泛指休息时间。例如：自从不久以前，美国粮食和药物管理局作出暂时停用隆胸原料矽液囊（矽胶）的决定之后，隆胸再次成为人们茶余饭后的话题。（《致命的吸引力》，1992年1月13日《联合早报》《现代生活》版）

"饭后"也说"酒后"。

Conversation After A Meal

Literally, this Chinese idiom means after tea or a meal. It refers to a hot topic which is being widely discussed by the public whenever they have the time.

Example: "Since the US Food and Drug Administration suspended the use of silicon for breast implant, the subject has become 'conversation after a meal'. " (Lianhe Zaobao 13/1/92)

成事不足，败事有余 chéng shì bùzú, bài shì yǒuyú

成事：办成事情；不足：没有办法或能力；败事：把事情
弄坏。指不能把事情办好，反而把事情办坏。也指不怀好意，
把本来可以办好的事情故意破坏掉。例如：戈尔巴乔夫上台六
年来究竟干了些什么？大体上有三种不同的看法……一部分人
认为：他成事不足，败事有余，好好一个国家给他弄成这么一
个破摊子。（《克里姆林宫出了新沙皇》，1991年12月27日
《联合早报》第15版）这个例句中，用的是第一个意思。

Unable To Accomplish Anything But Liable To Spoil Everything

This Chinese proverb is commonly used to describe a person
who is unhelpful and destructive.

Example: "What has Gorbachev contributed after being in
power for the past 6 years? There are conflicting views, but some feel
that he was 'unable to accomplish anything but liable to spoil every-
thing', making a mess of the country." (Lianhe Zaobao 27/12/91)

池鱼之殃 chí yú zhī yāng

池：护城河；殃：灾祸。比喻无缘无故受到连累。例如：正当台湾警方在台北一家麦当劳快餐店引爆第五枚炸弹的时候，台湾的肯德基家乡鸡快餐店为了避免遭受池鱼之殃，也宣布全岛35家分店暂时停止营业，直到爆炸案危机解除为止。（《歹徒警告肯德基是下一个目标，台肯德基分店昨起暂停营业》，1992年5月1日《联合早报》第23版）

也说成"池鱼遭殃"或"池鱼之祸"。跟这条成语同义的还有"城门失火，殃及池鱼"（因为偶然性的牵连而遭受祸害或损失）。

The Calamity Of The Fish In The Moat

This idiom comes from the proverb 'When the city gate catches fire, the fish in the moat suffer the calamity'. It means 'The suffering of the innocent bystanders'.

Example: "Following the detonation by the police of the fifth bomb found in a MacDonald's restaurant, Kentucky Fried Chicken announces that to avoid 'the calamity of the fish in the moat', all their 35 shops in Taiwan will be closed until further notice." (Lianhe Zaobao 1/5/92)

重蹈覆辙 chóng dǎo fù zhé

重：重复，再；蹈：踏上；覆：翻，倒；辙：车轮辗过的印儿。走上翻车的老路。比喻不吸取教训，重犯错误。例如：日本首相宫泽喜一打破数十年来的禁忌，昨天在国会就日本战时在亚洲邻国犯下的罪行，表示遗憾。

他说："我们必须正确教导历史，使我们时时警惕自己不要重蹈覆辙，同时要在国际社会负起我们应尽的责任。"（《对战时罪行，宫泽表遗憾》，1992年1月25日《联合早报》第2版）

也说"复蹈前辙"。

To Follow The Same Old Disastrous Road

Literally, this Chinese idiom means to follow the track of an overturned vehicle. It figuratively describes the failure to learn from another person's mistake.

Example: "Japanese PM Miyazawa discarded the decade-old tradition and openly expressed his contrition to Asian countries for his country's war crimes. He said Japan should learn from history and not 'to follow the same old disastrous road'. " (Lianhe Zaobao 25/1/92)

重作冯妇 chóng zuò Féngfù

重：再；作：当；冯妇：中国古代的勇士，善于打虎，后来决心不干了。一次他到野外去，看见一群人追捕老虎，就加入打虎的行列。比喻重新从事过去的职业或工作。例如：军人执政集团主席顺通，昨晚指责纳隆在没有征求其他政党领袖和全体国会议员同意之下仓促宣布组阁。他担心，纳隆的联合政府成员将出现一些不受欢迎的人物重作冯妇，而这个政府将不易受到国内外承认。（《顺通指责纳隆仓促组阁》，1992年3月26日《联合早报》第2版）

"重"也说"再"，"作"也说"当"。

To Become Fengfu Again

Fengfu was a brave and a skilled tiger hunter. He once vowed not to hunt tigers any more. Later, when he saw a tiger-hunting procession, he could not help but join in. This Chinese proverb describes a person going back to his former job or profession.

Example: "General Sunthorn Kongsompong, Thailand's junta chief, has criticised Mr Narong Wongwan for his hasty action in forming a new cabinet without consulting the leaders of other political parties and the members of parliament. General Sunthorn was worried that Mr Narong's coalition government might include some unwelcomed characters who are 'to become Fengfu again'. Such a government may not be acceptable both nationally and internationally." (Lianhe Zaobao 26/3/92)

出言不逊 chūyán bùxùn

出言：说话；不逊：没有礼貌/骄傲/蛮横。说话不客气，没有礼貌。例如：柔佛州移民厅局长那占那西前日说，今后凡是在新山长堤海关出言不逊、辱骂大马政府或移民厅官员的外国人，将被禁止进入大马。（《辱骂大马官员，外国人将被禁止入境》，1992年3月27日《联合早报》第2版）

To Make Impertinent Remarks

This Chinese idiom describes the way one speaks rudely, arrogantly, insolently or disdainfully.

Example: "Johor State Immigration director Mr Mohamed Nazam Nazir has said that foreigners who 'make impertinent remarks' at the Causeway checkpoint, hurl insults at Malaysia or the custom officers will be refused entry." (Lianhe Zaobao 27/3/92)

从善如流 cóng shàn rú liú

从善：听取好的、正确的意见；如流：像流水一样，比喻快。形容乐于接受别人好的、正确的意见。例如：在美世界旁边的空地建娱乐消闲设施，这是公众向市区重建局提出的建议。令人欣慰的是，该局从善如流，把这个建议纳入发展蓝图。（《公众提意见，公共部门从善如流》，1992年3月4日《联合早报》第3版）

"从"也说"纳"（采纳、接受）。

Readily Accept Good Advice

This Chinese idiom literally reads as "Follow good advice as naturally as a river follows its course."

Example: "The proposal to have recreational facilities at the vacant land next to The Beauty World was made by the general public. It is heartening to see that the authorities have 'followed good advice as naturally as a river follows its course' and have accepted and included the proposal in the Development Master Plan." (Lianhe Zaobao 4/3/92)

打草惊蛇　dǎ cǎo jīng shé

　　原来比喻惩罚张三，使李四受到警告。现多比喻做事不谨慎、不严密，事先惊动了对方，使对方有了防备。例如：如果在这个时候要一次过连根拔起，实际上就是打草惊蛇，在"十四大"之前让保守力量凝聚起来，这样做只会增加"十四大"时在人事方面更换的难度。（《中国七届人大五次会议前瞻》，1992年3月19日《联合早报》第17版）

To Beat The Grass And Frighten Away The Snake

　　This Chinese proverb originally means 'to punish one as a warning to the others'. But it is now more often used to mean 'to act rashly and thus unwittingly alert the enemy'.

　　Example: "To root out all the conservatives in one move would in fact amount to 'beating the grass and alerting the snakes'. The conservative forces could have pulled themselves together before the 14th CCP Congress. And it will only make it more difficult for the Congress to make any personnel changes." (Lianhe Zaobao 19/3/92)

大刀阔斧 dà dāo kuò fǔ

　　原指宽而大的刀、斧，是中国古代的两种兵器。现用来比喻办事果断而有魄力。例如：国家已经无路可走，我们不能一成不变，我们要大刀阔斧改变一切。（《戈尔巴乔夫辞职演讲》，1991年12月27日《联合早报》第30版）

To Take A Bold And Resolute Step

　　Literally, this Chinese idiom means to use a huge knife and broad-edged axe. It figuratively means to resort to some drastic measures.

　　Examples: "Gorbachev said that his country has already arrived at the end of the road and things cannot remained unchanged. It has to 'take a bold and resolute step' to reform." (Lianhe Zaobao 27/12/91)

大有作为 dà yǒu zuòwéi

作为：做出成绩，有贡献。形容能充分发挥才干，做出重大成绩。例如：云南风景秀丽，有发展旅游业的巨大潜能。李光耀先生在1988年9月访问昆明时就曾提起，随着新中两国航班次数的增加，新加坡人将能比过去较容易到西南省份去旅游和投资。

以新加坡人的国际贸易经验和市场联系网、管理才干，来开发仍是处女地的西南省份，必然会大有作为。（《符合产业政策的投资都受欢迎》，1992年1月8日《联合早报》第21版）

There Is Plenty Of Scope For Development

This Chinese idiom is commonly used to describe something, especially a person who has the potential to realise his talents fully or achieve great successes.

Example: "Yunnan province of China has beautiful sceneries and great potential for tourism. Mr Lee Kuan Yew mentioned during his visit there that with more air services, Singaporeans would find it more accessible and thus be able to help develop the place. 'There is plenty of scope for development'." (Lianhe Zaobao 8/1/92)

恩将仇报　ēn jiāng chóu bào

受了人家的恩惠，反而用仇恨来回报。

例如：中共曾派几十万军队参加韩战，与美国打了个平手，金日成也不像河内那样恩将仇报（尽管彼此之间也不是没有芥蒂），因此中共最高层一直很注意维持与金日成的关系。（《金日成父子的"只开放不改革"》，1992年5月4日《联合早报》第13版。芥蒂：jièdì，比喻心里的恶感或不快。）

To Requite Kindness With Enmity

This proverb describes behaviour that is more than ungrateful.

Example: "The Communist China had sent hundreds of thousands of troops to fight in the Korean War, and despite the unpleasantness that cropped up from time to time Kim II Song has never acted like Hanoi, 'to requite kindness with enmity.' That is why the top leadership of Communist China is maintaining close relations with Kim II Song." (Lianhe Zaobao 4/5/92)

耳熟能详 ěr shú néng xiáng

　　听得久了，熟悉了，也就能详尽地说出来。例如：王副总理也为歌唱名家潘秀琼伴奏经典名曲《不了情》，一唱一弹，那种耳熟能详、荡气回肠的旋律，立即在耳际飘荡。（《多位政坛名人高歌筹得270万元》，1992年5月4日《联合早报》第3版）

So Familiar To One's Ears That One Can Repeat In Detail

This adjectival idiom is used to describe words or sounds which are extremely familiar.

Example: "Deputy Prime Minister Ong accompanied the vocalist Pan Xiuqiong on the piano when she sang the song which had made her famous, the Endless Love. The soul-stirring melody 'so familiar to one's ears that one can repeat it in detail' reverberated beautifully in the air." (Lianhe Zaobao 4/5/92)

发扬光大 fāyáng guāngdà

发扬：发展和提倡；光大：辉煌、盛大。使美好的事物更加发展、提高。例如：因这一场误会而引起的辩论结果也是以"Win-Win"收场，辩论双方都是赢家。事实证明，华中"自强不息"的精神至今仍在校园内，甚至在校外发扬光大，"落伍校友"可以放心了。（《一个"美丽的误会"》，1992年1月12日《联合早报》第2版）

To Propagate It Widely

This Chinese idiom means to carry forward or promote the pioneering spirit or ideas of a person or organisation.

Example: "The controversy over the motto of Chinese High School ended up in a 'Win-Win' situation. This shows that the school's spirit is still being 'propagated widely' both inside and outside its campus." (Lianhe Zaobao 12/1/92)

风云人物　fēngyún rénwù

　　指在社会活动中影响很大的头面人物。例如：在1991年的圣诞节，世界各领袖纷纷发言赞扬前苏联的第一任也是最后一任总统戈尔巴乔夫是本世纪的一位伟大风云人物，其功绩将永垂青史。（《各国领袖赞老戈，功绩将永垂青史》，1991年12月27日《联合早报》第30版。垂：chuí，流传；青史：史书。）

Man Of The Hour

　　Literally, this Chinese idiom means a person who raises wind and clouds. It figuratively refers to people who are socially and politically very influential.

　　Example: "During the Christmas of 1991, Mr Gorbachev, who is the first as well as the last president of the former Soviet Union, was acclaimed by leaders around the world as the 'man of the hour', whose contributions would be honoured in history." (Lianhe Zaobao 27/12/91)

福星高照 fúxīng gāo zhào

福星：中国古代把木星叫做岁星，术士（求仙、炼丹的人）认为岁星所到的地方就会降福，因此又把木星叫做福星。后来把象征给人民带来幸福、希望的人或事物叫做福星，也用"福星高照"作为祝颂词语。例如：猴年开始不久，从报上看到香港某风水先生大胆预测：美国总统布斯、英国首相梅杰、俄罗斯总统耶尔辛，今年全会倒台，独中国最高领袖邓小平福星高照。（《老戈没有了，耶尔辛仍在》，1992年3月1日《联合早报》第2版）这句话是说邓小平不像布斯等人那样会倒运，他"福星高照"，今年会交好运。

Lucky Star Is Shining

In ancient China, planet Jupiter symbolised the star of longevity and happiness. It is now used in a complimentary sense to describe a person who is enjoying good fortune.

Example: "A HK fortune teller predicted that during the Year of the Monkey, President Bush, British PM John Major and Russian President Yeltsin would lose their power, only China's supreme leader Deng Xiaoping's 'lucky star will be shining'." (Lianhe Zaobao 1/3/92)

改弦易辙　gǎi xián yì zhé

弦：乐器上发声的线；易：更换；辙：车轮压下的痕迹，也指道路。乐器调换弦儿，车子改换道路。比喻改变方向、计划、做法或态度。例如：在国内，他（指戈尔巴乔夫）推行市场经济改革、引入多党政治；在国际上，苏联的外交改弦易辙，以和平取代对抗，放弃与美国进行多年的核子武器竞赛，结束了东西方的冷战时代。（《老戈完成其历史使命》），1991年12月27日《联合早报》社论）

"改"也说"更"（gēng，改变）

To Strike Out On A New Path

Literally, this Chinese idiom means to change the sound of the musical strings and to alter the track of the wheels. It figuratively infers a change in plan, method, attitude or direction.

Example: "Domestically, Gorbachev had implemented market economy and introduced a multi-party political system; internationally, he had 'struck out on a new path' in foreign policy and ended the arms race and the East-West Cold War." (Lianhe Zaobao 27/12/91)

高瞻远瞩 gāo zhān yuǎn zhǔ

瞻：向上或向前看；瞩：注意地看。看得高而远，形容目光远大。例如：布斯总统在2000名听众面前说："李资政，四分之一世纪以前，您领导这个多元文化、多元种族和缺乏资源的小岛取得独立。然后，凭着高瞻远瞩的眼光、智慧和毅力，您把新加坡塑造成一个国家……"（《布斯总统赞李资政将世世代代受人景仰》，1992年1月5日《联合早报》封面版）

To Take A Broad And Long-Term View

Literally, this Chinese idiom means to stand high and see far. It is used to describe someone who shows great foresight.

Example: "President Bush told the audience that Senior Minister Lee has led this multi-cultural, multi-racial, resource-scarce island to independence a quarter of a century ago. After this, he 'took a broad and long-term view', and with intelligence and determination, moulded Singapore into a nation.... ." (Lianhe Zaobao 5/1/92)

各自为政 gè zì wéi zhèng

为政：处理政事，泛指办事。各人按照自己的主张办事，不顾整体，也不跟别人配合协作。例如：政府要把新加坡建设成一个怎样的社会？一个属于新加坡人的新加坡，还是一个各族各自为政的新加坡？

新加坡民主党秘书长詹时中（波东巴西区议员）昨天在国会提出这样一个疑问，结果引起人民行动党的三名马来议员的驳斥。（《建设怎样的社会？》，1992年1月14日《联合早报》第8版）

To Go Their Separate Ways

This Chinese idiom describes people who conduct business in their own ways without cooperating with each other.

Example: "What kind of society is the government moulding Singapore into? A Singapore that belongs to Singaporeans or one with the different races 'going their separate ways'? These were questions posed by MP for Potong Pasir, Mr Chiam See Tong in Parliament and he was rebutted by three Malay PAP MPs." (Lianhe Zaobao 14/1/92)

故步自封 gù bù zì fēng

故步：原来走的步子，引申为旧办法或老一套；自封：自己限制自己，停留在原地。比喻对目前的情况很满足，不求创新进取。例如：东欧共党政权接二连三垮台，苏共解散，苏联解体，都对故步自封的朝鲜金日成父子带来巨大的冲击，使他们面临前所未有的生存危机。（《金日成父子的"只开放不改革"》，1992年5月4日《联合早报》第13版）

"故"也写成"固"。

To Follow One's Own Old Steps And Be Self-Conceited

This proverb means 'To be complacent and conservative'.

Example: "The collapse of the communist regimes one after another in Eastern Europe, the dissolution of the Russian Communist Party and the disintegration of the Soviet Union have badly affected Kim II Song and his son in North Korea who 'have been following their own old steps and becoming self-conceited'. They are now facing an unprecedented crisis of survival." (Lianhe Zaobao 4/5/92)

刮目相看　guā mù xiāng kàn

　　刮目：擦眼睛，指改变过去的看法。指别人已有显著的进步，要用新的眼光来看待。例如：新加坡国际基金会会长陈庆珠教授说，成功地取得经济发展的国家，肯定会得到其他国家的尊敬和重视。在这方面，新加坡已进入令人刮目相看的时期。（《新加坡的发展令人刮目相看》，1992年3月29日《联合早报》第4版）

　　"看"也说"待"。

To Remove The Scales From One's Eyes Before Looking At Someone

This Chinese proverb means the subject has made marked improvement and should be looked upon in a new and favourable light.

Example: "Prof Chan Heng Chee, Executive Director of SIF says that a country which is successful in economic development will surely be highly regarded and respected by the others. Singapore is now entering a stage where the others have 'to remove the scales from their eyes before looking at it'." (Lianhe Zaobao 29/3/92)

海阔天空　hǎi kuò tiān kōng

　　像海一样辽阔，像天一样没有边际。比喻在广阔的天地里，可以充分施展抱负，大显身手。例如：旅馆业培训中心主任张宝琴说："学生取得的文凭，就像一把帮助他们打开事业大门的钥匙。入了行，这个行业海阔天空，任由他们发展。"（《一把钥匙天地宽》，1992年4月7日《联合早报》第7版）

　　"海"也说成"水"，"空"也说成"高"。

As Boundless As The Sea And Sky

　　This Chinese proverb figuratively describes something that is unrestrained and far-ranging.

　　Example: "Director of Hotel Operation Training Centre, Ms Zhang Baoqin says that the certificate is a key which will help the students open up a career in the industry. And this is an industry 'as boundless as the sea and sky' for them to develop themselves." (Lianhe Zaobao 7/4/92)

洪水猛兽 hóngshuǐ měngshòu

洪水：可能造成灾害的大水；猛兽：凶猛的会伤害人或其他动物的野兽。比喻极大的祸害。例如：这次邓小平也不客气，干脆承认改革开放就是要把资本主义的有些东西引入中国，而且用错了也不要紧。这一番话打破了两年多来中国的另一个政治禁忌。资本主义不再是洪水猛兽，甚至还有它十分可爱的一面。（《邓小平从幕后走向台前》，1992年1月31日《联合早报》第18版）

Dreadful Floods And Savage Beasts

Horrendous floods and wild beasts have long been great scourges that threatened human life. This Chinese idiom is used figuratively to describe great disasters.

Example: "This time, Deng Xiaoping is very straight-forward. He said bluntly that economic reforms is to introduce certain good practices of capitalism to China. Thus, capitalism is no longer 'dreadful floods and savage beasts', but something that might be welcomed." (Lianhe Zaobao 31/1/92)

化为乌有 huà wéi wūyǒu

乌有：无、没有。变得什么都没有，形容全部丧失或完全落空。例如：卢布汇价自由浮动，黑市汇价变成市价，这意味着前苏联政府数十年来欠下人民的钱（债券）及人民的储蓄6000亿卢布，一夜之间几乎化为乌有。（《戈尔巴乔夫不能，耶尔辛也不能》，1992年1月2日《联合早报》第13版）

To Melt Into Thin Air

This Chinese idiom describes something that has come to naught or simply vanished.

Example: "By allowing the rouble to float, its exchange rate in the black market has become the official rate. This means that the money the former Soviet Union government owed its people in the form of bonds, and the people's 600 billion roubles in savings have all 'melted into thin air'." (Lianhe Zaobao 2/1/92)

浑身解数　húnshēn xièshù

浑身：全身；解数：武术的架势、路数。指全身的本事或所有的本领。例如：中国书法和国画的买主，绝大多数是华侨、港澳台人士，外国人则以日本人为主。整个中国画市场是供大于求，因此各经销单位不惜使出浑身解数，竞相招引顾客。（《中国画的"生意经"》，1992年3月12日《联合早报》第21版）

All One's Skills

Literally, this Chinese idiom refers to all the movements in martial arts one is good in.

Example: "Most potential buyers of Chinese painting and calligraphy are overseas Chinese and Japanese. In fact, the supply far exceeds the demand. That is why all the sales agents of Chinese art have to bring all their skills into play to compete in the market." (Lianhe Zaobao 12/3/92)

火冒三丈 huǒ mào sān zhàng

冒：往上升。形容十分生气。例如：耶尔辛在《直言札记》一书中忆述："在政治局会议中，我们曾预先讨论戈尔巴乔夫在十月革命70周年纪念日的演说。我对演词提出了10点批评，令他（指戈尔巴乔夫）很愤怒。这也使我火冒三丈，我记得我很不以为然，为什么一个人对别人的批评会有如此近乎歇斯底里的反应。"（《戈耶积怨由来》，1991年12月27日《联合早报》第15版）

Raising The Fire Of Fury

Literally, it means the fire of fury rises up to three 'zhang' (one zhang is 3.33 metres). It is used to describe a person who is burning with anger.

Example: "In his book, Yeltsin says that when he criticised Gorbachev's speech at the 70th anniversary of The Revolution, Gorbachev was very angry. And this also made him 'raise his fire of fury'. Why should a person be so hysterical when criticised?" (Lianhe Zaobao 27/12/1991)

驾轻就熟 *jià qīng jiù shú*

驾：赶马车；轻：轻快的车；就：走上；熟：熟路。赶着轻车走熟路。比喻对事情很熟悉，做起来容易。例如：刘琦说，培训模特儿是她的老本行，做起来驾轻就熟，而且在培训中还能发现许多有潜质的新人，得到很大的满足感。（《刘琦伴着闲话过日子》，1992年3月26日《联合早报》《影艺》版）

也说成"轻车熟路"。

To Drive A Light Carriage On A Familiar Road

This Chinese proverb figuratively describes one who does a familiar job with great ease.

Example: "Liu Qi said the job of training models used to be her line. She can do it like 'driving a light carriage on a familiar road'. She would also get the satisfaction of cultivating new talents with potential." (Lianhe Zaobao 26/3/92)

剑拔弩张 jiàn bá nǔ zhāng

弩：射箭的弓；张开。剑从鞘（qiào，装刀、剑的套子）里拔出来了，弓也张开了。形容形势十分紧张，一触即发（yī chù jí fā，成语，一碰就发作）。例如：最近，好几个会馆的内部争执表面化，几乎已经成为街谈巷议的材料。有的会馆在竞选或举行大会之前，从前那种一团和气相互谦让（qiānràng）的作风，变为剑拔弩张互不相让的场面。（《会馆需要"鲁仲连"吗？》，1992年4月14日《联合早报》社论。街谈巷议：jiētán xiàngyì，成语，大街小巷里人们的议论。一团和气：yī tuán héqì，成语，指和睦（mù）相处。）

With Swords Drawn And Bows Bent

This proverb figuratively describes a situation where a clash is about to take place.

Example: "Recently, the internal disputes in a few clan associations have come to the surface. At the recent election session of several associations, the traditional friendly and amicable atmosphere with everybody modestly declining high office had vanished. Instead, it was as if there were 'swords drawn and bows bent'." (Lianhe Zaobao 14/4/92)

江河日下 jiāng hé rì xià

　　江河的水天天向下游流去。比喻事物一天天地衰落或情况一天天地恶化。例如："厚着脸皮为衰退的美国经济充当推销员，一个在国内声望江河日下的总统，作绝望的挣扎。"这就是昨天日本的传播媒介对美国布斯总统的写照。（《日本报章挖苦布斯，厚脸皮推销员》，1992年1月9日《联合早报》第32版）

To Be On The Decline

　　Literally, this Chinese idiom describes the flow of the river which is flowing downward day after day. It is used figuratively to refer to something which is going from bad to worse.

　　Example: "The Japanese mass media profiled President Bush as a brazen salesman struggling for a faltering economy whose country's reputation is "on the decline". (Lianhe Zaobao 9/1/92)

叫苦连天 jiàokǔ liántiān

叫苦：诉说苦处；连天：连续不间断。不断叫苦，形容痛苦得很。例如：学校的测验题与考题越来越难，甚至出了一些原是高班级教学范围内的题目。有些班只有少数学生及格，大部分学生叫苦连天。（《揠苗助长，弊多于利》，1992年3月28日《联合早报》第14版）

To Groan Or Complain Incessantly

This Chinese idiom figuratively describes the feeling of severe pain or suffering.

Example: "The questions in the school examination and test papers have been getting more and more difficult. Some of them were even set against the syllabi of a higher level. In some classes, only a few students managed to pass while the majority of them could only 'moan and groan incessantly'." (Lianhe Zaobao 28/3/92)

节外生枝　jié wài shēng zhī

　　在原来枝节上又生出新的枝节。比喻在原有的问题之外，又生出新的问题；也比喻故意制造麻烦，使事情不能顺利进行。例如：大马全国警察总长韩聂夫昨天透露，如果没有节外生枝的话，另一批前马共成员预料今年3月会回大马定居。（《另一批前马共成员，预料三月可回大马》，1992年1月23日《联合早报》第11版）

　　"节外"也说"节上"。

A Branch Growing Out Of A Tree Joint

　　This Chinese idiom refers to side issues or new problems which crop up unexpectedly. It usually refers to unnecessary difficulties caused by someone sabotaging a plan.

　　Example: "Malaysian Chief of Police, Mr Haniff said that unless there is 'a branch growing out of the tree joint', another batch of ex-Malayan Communist Party members should be able to return to settle in the country in March." (Lianhe Zaobao 23/1/92)

精益求精 jīng yì qiú jīng

精：完美；益：更加；求：追求。好了还要求更好，永远
没有止境。例如：白清泉说："战场上打仗讲求战略和战术，
推销酱油则靠策划和经验。做生意也和打仗一样，要不断收集
完整的市场资料，不断精益求精，才能得胜。"（《本地酱油
"进军"国际》，1992年1月3日《联合早报》第23版）

To Constantly Strive For Improvement

"Jing" means excellence. This Chinese idiom means to achieve
excellence by continually improving oneself.

Example: "Mr Peh Cheng Chua said that in warfare, it's military
strategy that counts; whereas in business, it depends on planning and
experience. Business is similar to warfare. We have to collect market
information and 'constantly strive for improvement' before we can
win the battle." (Lianhe Zaobao 3/1/92)

举棋不定 jǔ qí bù dìng

拿起棋子不知道走哪一着（zhāo）才好。比喻遇到事情犹豫不决，拿不定主意。例如：耶尔辛在政策上举棋不定，对民主政治缺乏了解，对市场经济缺乏常识与经验，对此，俄罗斯及西方政坛人士很担心。（《耶尔辛将把俄罗斯推进危局》，1992年3月4日《联合早报》第11版）

Hold A Chessman And Vacillate

This Chinese proverb uses one's hesitation in making a move in a chess game to illustrate a state of mind which can be described as shilly-shally.

Example: "The fact that Boris Yeltsin used 'to hold a chessman and vacillate' in policy-making, and does not understand how a democracy works, in addition to his lack of knowledge of and experience in market economy makes the Russians and Western politicians worried." (Lianhe Zaobao 12/3/92)

举足轻重 jǔ zú qīng zhòng

形容所处的地位十分重要，一举一动都关系到大局。例如：国家经济体制改革委员会是中国国务院的一个部委机构，统筹策划、协调、研究、引导全国的经济体制改革工作，在国家改革开放的过程中扮演着举足轻重的角色。（《符合产业政策的投资都受欢迎》，1992年1月8日《联合早报》第21版）

"轻重"也说"重轻"。

To Occupy A Decisive Position

This Chinese idiom literally means by lifting one's leg, one can tip the scales. It is used to describe a person who holds the balance in a particular situation.

Example: "The National Economic Reform Commission is an important body under China's State Council. It is responsible for planning, coordinating and directing various economic functions. In the country's open door policy, it 'occupies a decisive position'." (Lianhe Zaobao 8/1/92)

聚沙成塔 jù shā chéng tǎ

把細沙堆积成宝塔，比喻积少成多。例如：一般上，银行减低贷款利率的同时，也会降低存款的利率，这一减一降的幅度如果一样，银行的利润看来还是保持不变，可是一些小小的差距还是有的。别小看这小小的差距，聚沙成塔的利润仍然是十分可观的。（《减息宜速》，1991年12月28日《联合早报》第23版）

Piling Sand Into A Pagoda

This Chinese idiom's English equivalent is "Many a little makes a mickle".

Example: "Generally, when banks reduce their prime rates, they will lower interest rates for savings at the same time. If both move in tandem, their profits will remain unchanged. However, there is usually a slight difference. The amount may be small, but by 'piling sand into a pagoda', the total sum may be quite substantial." (Lianhe Zaobao 28/12/91)

开诚布公 kāi chéng bù gōng

开诚：敞开胸怀，显示诚意；布：宣布。揭示内心的想法，提出公正的见解。形容发表或交换意见时态度诚恳，坦白无私，真诚坦率地谈出自己的看法。例如：政府可以在不公开言明的情况下作出决定，或甚至事后在受人质疑时加以否认。然而，吴总理却选择了不同的方式，即把这种作法预先公开出来，以显示他个人喜欢开诚布公的作风。（《开诚布公的施政作风》，1992年4月22日《联合早报》社论）

也说"推诚布公"，"推诚"：以诚心实意待人。

Open, Sincere And Expressively Fair

This idiom describes the frank, sincere, unreserved and unselfish way in which one makes clear his thinking.

Example: "The government can make a decision without making it public and can even deny it when it is questioned. But PM Goh prefers a different way, that is, to make known before implementation to show his preference for an 'open, sincere, and expressively fair' style." (Lianhe Zaobao 22/4/92)

空空如也 kōngkōng rú yě

原本的意思是内心空虚的样子。现形容空空的什么也没有。例如：从新闻照片上看到莫斯科居民在空空如也的商店前排长龙的愤怒表情，再目睹北京大小商店货物充足、人们任意选购的热闹情况，就不难知道为什么戈尔巴乔夫的改革开放把苏联的命都给革掉了，邓小平的改革开放却仍然能维持一片稳定的景象，坚持要继续走"具有中国特色的社会主义道路"。（《从国情看中国的改革》，1992年1月8日《联合早报》第21版）

Absolutely Empty

This Chinese idiom is usually used to describe a place or a container that has nothing inside at all.

Example: "From the photos published in newspapers, it can be seen that shops in Moscow are 'absolutely empty' as shoppers queue angrily outside. On the other hand, shops in Beijing are filled with goods allowing customers to choose freely. The contrast shows clearly that Gorbachev's reform has obviously failed." (Lianhe Zaobao 8/1/92)

快刀斩乱麻　kuài dāo zhǎn luàn má

比喻果断快捷地解决复杂的问题。例如：尽管不久前地铁公司大事张扬香口胶对地铁车厢所造成的污化，甚至说地铁公司的正常服务也受到影响，政府的香口胶禁令还是来得非常突然。政府这次表现出快刀斩乱麻式的行事作风，让有关的商家措手不及，也使得公众来不及提出反对或是保留意见。（《咀嚼香口胶禁令的余味》，1992年1月8日《联合早报》第20版。措手不及：cuò shǒu bù jí，成语，临时来不及应付。）

To Cut The Gordian Knot

Literally, this Chinese idiom means to cut a tangled skein of jute with a sharp knife. It describes a decisive action to resolve a complex problem.

Example: "Although the MRTC had recently cried out loudly about how chewing gum dirtied its stations and disrupted its services, few expected the ban to have come so swiftly. The government's act 'to cut the Gordian knot' caught the public and businessmen by surprise." (Lianhe Zaobao 8/1/92)

了若指掌 liǎo ruò zhǐ zhǎng

了：了解、明白；指掌：指着手掌。对情况清楚得就像指点手掌上的东西给人家看一样。比喻对情况了解得非常清楚。例如：丹那巴南部长对他须要应付的课题，从建筑工程管制，到建筑业客工的供应，从组屋翻新，到社区设施的改进，从组屋售价高涨，到行人天桥的建造等等，都了若指掌。（《詹时中忘了！》，1992年3月12日《联合早报》第8版）

"若"也说"如"。

Know Something Like It Is In The Palm

This Chinese proverb means literally that one knows something so well it is as if he is holding it in the palm and showing it to others.

Example: "Mr S Dhanabalan knew all the subjects he had to deal with so well 'like they were something held in his palm and he was just pointing it out to others'. The subjects ranged from the control over building projects to the supply of foreign construction labourers, from upgrading of HDB flats to improvement of community services and from the soaring resale price of HDB flats to the construction of pedestrain flyovers." (Lianhe Zaobao 12/3/92)

落花流水 luò huā liú shuǐ

　　落下的花瓣儿随着流水飘走，原本形容春天将要过去时花儿凋零的景象。现多用来比喻被打得大败。例如：去年2月26日，布斯总统获悉联军在"沙漠风暴"行动中把入侵科威特的伊拉克军打得落花流水之后，就被一个问题困扰：这场仗该打到什么地方和什么时候为止？（《波斯湾战争太早结束？》，1992年1月17日《联合早报》第32版）

　　也可以倒过来说成"流水落花"。

Like Fallen Flowers Carried Away By The Flowing River

　　This Chinese idiom describes fallen flower petals being carried away by the currents in the river. It figuratively means something which has been totally destroyed or utterly routed.

　　Example: "Last year, when President Bush received news that US troops had 'utterly routed' the Iraqi soldiers in Kuwait, he was troubled by the question of how long and how far his troops should advance in the war." (Lianhe Zaobao 17/1/92)

美中不足 měi zhōng bùzú

美：好。指事情虽然好，但是还有不够的地方。例如：这一次A水准会考放榜唯一美中不足的地方，就是某些初级学院觉得有需要联合起来不向报界发布会考成绩。（《有竞争，才会有进步》，1992年3月10日《联合早报》社论）

A Blemish In An Otherwise Perfect Thing

The English equivalence of this Chinese proverb is 'a fly in the ointment'.

Example: "There was 'a blemish in an otherwise perfect thing' when the results of 1991 "A" level Examination were released recently. A number of junior colleges collectively thought it necessary to withhold from the press their results." (Lianhe Zaobao 10/3/92)

平起平坐　píng qǐ píng zuò

比喻双方地位平等。例如：大马首相马哈迪医生说，在经济与民族都强大时，大马就可以跟先进国平起平坐，不必向他们低头祈求。（《马哈迪：要与先进国平起平坐，马须先巩固经济力量》，《联合早报》1992年3月24日第11版）

To Sit And Stand Up As Equals

This Chinese proverb means 'On equal footing' or 'Of same status'.

Example: "Malaysian Prime Minister Dr Mahathir Mohamad said that when the nation and its economy become strong, Malaysia would then be in the position 'to sit and stand up as equals' with the developed nations and not have to bow to them any more." (Lianhe Zaobao 24/3/92)

迫不得已 pò bù dé yǐ

迫：逼迫。指被情势逼迫，没有办法，不得不这样。例如：一架单引擎（engine）飞机在飞行中，机师心脏病发作而突然死亡，机内一名搭客迫不得已充当机师，在另一架并排飞行的飞机的指导员指示下，他好不容易把飞机安全降落在机场。（《机师死亡乘客驾机，有惊无险安全着陆》，1992年4月2日《联合早报》第30版）

Be Forced To

This Chinese idiom is used to describe a situation in which one has no alternative but to do something in spite of himself.

Example: "The pilot of a single-engined aeroplane died suddenly of a heart attack during the flight. One passenger 'was forced to' take the pilot's seat, and under the guidance of a pilot flying another plane next to his, managed to land the plane safely on the airstrip." (Lianhe Zaobao 2/4/92)

破镜重圆　pò jìng chóng yuán

比喻夫妻决裂或失散后，重又和好、团聚。例如：柬埔寨战争结束，为区域发展稳定及和平制造了机会，并为中国和越南关系正常化排除了障碍。其实，自苏联共产党瓦解后，越南就已设法要与中国破镜重圆。（《越南发奋图强》，1992年1月4日《联合早报》第15版）

中越两国曾有过一个蜜月时期，后来两国关系恶化甚至打了起来。现在两国关系已经正常化，因此作者用"破镜重圆"来形容。

A Broken Mirror Rejoined

This Chinese idiom usually refers to the reunion of husband and wife after an enforced separation.

Example: "The ending of the Cambodian war brought stability to the region and has removed the barrier between China and Vietnam to restore mutual relations. As a matter of fact, since the collapse of the Soviet Union, Vietnam has tried hard to 'rejoin the broken mirror'." (Lianhe Zaobao 4/1/91)

七上八下 qī shàng bā xià

形容心情起伏不定，心中慌乱、不安。例如：今年的前三个月，由于刚刚到一个完全陌生的环境上课，所以心里总是七上八下，没一点安全感。（《走过1991·浪漫的相遇》，1991年12月31日《联合早报》《少男少女》版）

"下"也说"落"。

"七上八下"常跟在"十五个吊桶打水"之后连着说，构成歇后语。

To Be Ill At Ease

This Chinese idiom describes the feeling of agitation.

Example: "During the first three months of the year, I had to attend a course in a totally unfamiliar surrounding. It made me feel 'ill at ease' and insecure." (Lianhe Zaobao 31/12/1991)

旗开得胜　qí kāi dé shèng

　　旗：军旗；开：展开。军旗一展开就打了胜仗。比喻事情刚开始做就获得成功。例如：布斯首次当"超级汽车推销员"，就旗开得胜，成绩非凡，确是应该庆幸。（《"推销员"晕倒日本首相府》，1992年1月12日《联合早报》第2版）

　　"得胜"也说"取胜"。

Victory At The Outset

This Chinese idiom means to achieve victory at the very beginning of the battle. It is used to compliment someone who achieves a speedy success.

Example: "President Bush has turned himself into a super car salesman. He scored 'a victory at the outset' and achieved impressive results. He is indeed to be congratulated." (Lianhe Zaobao 12/1/92)

杞人忧天 Qǐ rén yōu tiān

杞：中国古代国名，在现今的河南省杞县。传说杞国有个人担心天会塌下来，愁得觉也不睡，饭也不吃。比喻不必要的或缺乏根据的忧虑。例如：各国担心前苏联的核子技术专家会在高薪和利诱之下流到其他发展中国家去，并非"杞人忧天"。（《核子强国的共同任务》，1992年1月31日《联合早报》社论）

To Entertain Groundless Fears

Literally, this Chinese idiom means the man of Qi who was haunted by the fear that the sky might fall. It is used to describe people who worry unnecessarily.

Example: "Various nations are worried that nuclear experts of the former Soviet Union may be enticed by high salaries to work for the Third World countries. Indeed, they are not 'entertaining groundless fears'." (Lianhe Zaobao 31/1/92)

千丝万缕 qiān sī wàn lǚ

缕：线。千条丝，万条线，形容彼此之间关系密切、复杂，难以割断。例如：新山一些人认为，新马两地的关系一向都相当密切，尤其是新山市民与新加坡人的关系更是千丝万缕，历史的因素造成两地许多人有着血浓于水的关系。（《新山总商会会长刘南辉：指新加坡人造成柔通膨，只是新山少数市民看法》，1992年4月22日《联合早报》第2版）

也说"万缕千丝"。

Thousands of Strands

The idiom figuratively describes something that is made of so many complicated and intricately intertwining elements, a simple solution is out of the question.

Example: "Some people in Johor Bahru think that all along, the relations between Singapore and Malaysia have been so close, particularly, the links between Singaporeans and Johoreans which are like 'thousands of strands'. Historical factors have helped many people in these two territories build a tie that can be described as 'blood is thicker than water'." (Lianhe Zaobao 22/4/92)

黔驴技穷 Qián lǘ jì qióng

黔：中国贵州省别称；穷：尽，完了。贵州本来没有驴，有人带了一头去，放在山下牧养。老虎见驴个子很大，又听到它叫声很响，起初很害怕。后来经过观察，觉得驴并没有什么特别的本领，就靠近它，最后把它吃了（柳宗元：《三戒·黔之驴》）。比喻有限的一点儿本领也用完了。例如：戈尔巴乔夫走到如此地步，苏联走到如此地步，以美国为首的西方要不要负一定责任？如果不是西方一而再、再而三地强迫戈尔巴乔夫加速改革，如果不是戈尔巴乔夫一而再、再而三地进行迎合西方需要的改革，或许也不会跌得如此之惨，而被耶尔辛扫地出门。

美国和西方国家目前是黔驴技穷，骑虎难下，怎么办？只有骑驴看唱本，走着瞧了。（《克里姆林宫出了新沙皇》，1991年12月27日《联合早报》第15版）

One Who Has Exhausted His Tricks

This Chinese idiom originated from a proverbial donkey who tried to show off his skills when confronted by a tiger. It was eventually eaten up. It is now used to describe one who is rather helpless when faced with real difficulties.

Example: "The US and European countries have put pressure on Gorbachev to reform. Now that he has been driven into a totally hopeless situation, the western countries 'have also exhausted their tricks'." (Lianhe Zaobao 27/12/91)

秦庭哭师 Qín tíng kū shī

庭：朝廷。公元前506年，吴国进攻楚国，楚国大败，就派大臣申包胥（xū）到秦国去求救。申包胥在秦国的朝廷靠着墙哭了七天七夜，终于感动了秦哀公，于是派兵去救楚国，打退了吴国的军队。比喻苦苦地哀求别人的援助。例如：一月底，耶尔辛赴新大陆秦庭哭师，他的座机刚在莫斯科机场升空，鲁特斯科伊便在前苏共机关报《真理报》上发难，发表攻击耶尔辛的文章。（《俄罗斯政变谣传的内幕》，1992年2月20日《联合早报》第13版）

To Cry For Help

This Chinese idiom refers to an official of the Chu State in the Warring States Period in China. When Chu was attacked by Wu, the official, Shen Baoxu sought help from Qin. He cried for 7 days and 7 nights at the Qin Court before his request was granted.

Example: "In January, Yeltsin went to America 'to cry for help'. When his plane had barely left Moscow Airport, his critics started to attack him." (Lianhe Zaobao 20/2/92)

青黄不接 qīng huáng bù jiē

青：田里的青苗；黄：成熟的谷物。陈粮已经吃完，新谷还没有成熟。比喻人力、物力或财力暂时中断，接续不上。例如：一些会馆目前正处在新旧交替之时，另一些则可能正处在青黄不接的阶段，某些人事上的冲突或者看法上的差异，可能无法避免，从积极角度来看，不同意见或者竞争的出现，也不一定就是坏事。（《会馆需要"鲁仲连"吗？》，1992年4月14日《联合早报》社论）

"不接"也说"未接"或"不交"（交：相连接）。

The Green And Yellow Do Not Join

Green stands for the new crop which is still in the blade. Yellow is the old one. This proverb figuratively describes a discontinuity in replacement or succession.

Example: "Some clan associations are in the process of renewal, some probably in the state of 'the green and yellow do not join'. A few incidents of personality clash or disagreement are therefore inevitable. However, it is not necessarily bad to have some disagreement and competition." (Lianhe Zaobao 14/4/92)

绳之以法　shéng zhī yǐ fǎ

绳：准绳，比喻言论、行动等所依据的原则或标准；当动词用，可当"约束"讲。之：代词，代替受到约束或制裁的对象。以：用。用法律来约束，按刑法来制裁。例如：金文泰警署署长林汉辉警监昨日颁赠表扬状给护理员俞月明时，赞扬她机智尽责，使警方能迅速将窃贼绳之以法。（《护理员机警尽责，助警迅速破案获表扬》，1992年3月1日《联合早报》第4版）

也说"以法绳之"。

To Enforce Law Upon Someone

This Chinese idiom means to have one's conduct and speech restrained by law.

Example: "The head of the Clementi Police Station, superintendent Lin Hanhui presented a letter of Commendation to nurse Yu Yueming, praising her for her quick-wittedness and strong sense of duty, which enabled the police 'to enforce the law upon' the thieves." (Lianhe Zaobao 1/3/92)

十八层地狱 shí bā céng dìyù

佛教认为，人活着做坏事，死了就要受报应，掉进第十八层最阴惨的地狱，永远没有翻身的日子。比喻最黑暗、最痛苦的境地。这条成语常跟"打入"连用。例如：史大林去见马克思以后，克鲁雪夫曾设法把进入死胡同的北极熊提出来，结果顽固保守的布列兹涅夫又把它打入十八层地狱。等到戈尔巴乔夫下手抢救时，已经太晚了。（《回顾苏联的兴与亡》，1992年1月31日《联合早报》第15版）

To Banish It To The 18th Level Of Hell

In Buddhism, it is believed that there are 18 levels in hell and the lowest being the darkest and harshest place where the condemned are beyond redemption.

Example: "After Stalin had gone to see Marx, Khrushchev tried to get the troubled polar bear out of the dead road. But Brezhnev, the stubborn conservative 'banished it to the 18th level of hell'. By the time Gorbachev tried to save it, it was already too late." (Lianhe Zaobao 31/1/92)

识途老马 shí tú lǎo mǎ

也说"老马识途",老马能够认识路。比喻经验丰富的人,对情况很熟悉。例如:同行的"识途老马"告诉我,越南的蕃薯,味道特别甜,特别好吃,在越南期间,不要错过机会。(《什么生意可以做?》,1992年2月17日《联合早报》第17版)

An Old Horse Who Knows The Way

It is used figuratively to describe a person who is experienced and knowledgeable. Its English equivalent is "A wise old bird".

Example: "My colleague, 'an old horse who knows the way' told me that the sweet potato in Vietnam was unusually delicious and asked me not to miss it while travelling in the country." (Lianhe Zaobao 17/2/92)

寿终正寝 shòu zhōng zhèng qǐn

寿终：很大年纪才去世；正寝：旧式住宅的正房。指老人死在家里。比喻事物的消亡。例如：R级片放映的第一天，几乎每家电影院都场场爆满。原本用意很好的措施，却因一些唯利是图的片商一窝蜂地推出低级色情电影，而使当局修订了条例，这类R级电影也就寿终正寝了。（《走过1991·一起闯R关》，1991年12月31日《联合早报》《少男少女》版）

To Die A Natural Death

This Chinese idiom is commonly used to describe a person who dies of old age. It is also used to refer to something that has come to an end.

Example: "When R-rated films were first introduced, all the cinema operators rushed to screen them to make a quick buck. But the government's change in regulations arrested the influx of soft-porn movies. The result is that R-rated films 'died a natural death'." (Lianhe Zaobao31/12/91)

树大招风　shù dà zhāo fēng

比喻名声大或地位高的人，容易惹人注意而担风险或被妒忌（dùjì）。例如：当红偶像黎明真可谓树大招风，经常都有不利他的新闻传出。不久前就有一家周刊说，他与周海媚在酒店闹翻。（《黎明树大招风，不利谣言四处飞》，1991年12月23日《联合早报》《影艺》版）

"大"也说"高"。

A Tall Tree Catches The Wind

This Chinese idiom is used to figuratively illustrate the fact that people in high positions are more likely to face risks or be attacked by others.

Example: "As a public idol, Li Ming is indeed like 'a tall tree which catches the wind'. There are scandalous rumours about him from time to time. Sometime ago, a weekly publication reported that he quarrelled with Zhou Haimei in a hotel." (Lianhe Zaobao 23/12/91)

树欲静而风不止　shù yù jìng ér fēng bù zhǐ

这条成语的下一句是"子欲养而亲不待"，意思是子女想奉养父母而父母早已去世，不能如愿以偿。树想静下来，风却不停地吹，因此树就不得不动起来。比喻客观情势是不以人的意志为转移的。例如：树欲静而风不止。从1983年《我的路》出版到现在，已经整整八年了。八年来，我虽然没有提笔再写一个字，可是我的生活及事业的动荡却越来越激烈，谣言工厂目不转睛地继续瞄准我这个靶子，制造出一串一串不同的传闻。（《我为什么要再写自传》，1992年5月1日《联合早报》《茶馆》版。目不转睛：mùbùzhuǎnjīng，成语，形容注意力很集中，看得出神。）

The Tree May Prefer Calm, But The Wind Will Not Subside

The second half of this proverb reads as 'Children may want to support, but the parents are gone'. The meaning is, 'Will cannot change the course on nature or events'.

Example: "I (film star Liu Xiaoqing) have not written a word for the last eight years. 'The tree may prefer calm, but the wind will not subside', the turbulence in my career and my life has gone from bad to worse. Rumours are constantly being targetted at me." (Lianhe Zaobao 1/5/92)

水火不相容　shuǐ huǒ bù xiāng róng

容：容纳。比喻双方对立，互不相容，不能共处。例如：香港汇丰银行较早时宣布，将收购英国四大银行之一的米特兰银行。可是，英国另一家大银行劳埃特银行昨日正式提出敌意收购米特兰。现在的形势是，汇丰与劳埃特为争夺米特兰弄得水火不相容。（《劳埃特与汇丰"决一死战"》，1992年4月29日《联合早报》第22版）

也说"水火不同炉"。

To Be As Incompatible As Fire And Water

This idiom figuratively describes the incompatibility of two things diametrically opposed to each other.

Example: "Lloyds Bank has made a takeover bid for Midland Bank after HSBC. Now, the two banks which are vying for Midland Bank 'are as incompatible as fire and water' to each other." (Lianhe Zaobao 29/4/92)

水乳交融 shuǐ rǔ jiāo róng

水乳：水和乳汁；交融：融合在一起。比喻关系十分融洽（róngqià）或结合得十分紧密。例如：欧进福博士不但是一名受过高深教育的学者，也是一名与民间基层水乳交融的代议士。（《争取不会讲英语的人提意见》，1992年3月28日《联合早报》社论）

As Well Blended As Milk And Water

This Chinese idiom figuratively describes a relationship of complete harmony.

Example: "Dr Ow Chin Hock is not only a highly educated scholar but also a people's representative whose relationship with the grassroots is 'as well blended as milk and water'." (Lianhe Zaobao 28/3/92)

水泄不通　shuǐ xiè bù tōng

　　泄：排泄。水都流不出去。形容十分拥挤或包围、封锁、控制得非常严密。例如：元旦前夕，俄罗斯人民纷纷涌上街头去排队，购买面包和其他生活必需品。所有的商店都被蜂拥而来的顾客挤得水泄不通。（《独联解除物价控制，津贴取消，物价将飞涨》，1992年1月2日《联合早报》封面版）这个例句中的"水泄不通"形容十分拥挤。

Not Even A Drop Of Water Can Trickle Through

　　This Chinese idiom describes a situation which is watertight or jam-packed.

　　Example: "On New Year's eve, the Russians queued along the streets to buy bread and other necessities. All the shops were so packed with customers 'not even a drop of water could trickle through'." (Lianhe Zaobao 2/1/92)

顺手牵羊 shùn shǒu qiān yáng

顺手把人家的羊牵走。比喻乘便拿走人家的东西。例如：染上偷窃癖（Kleptomania）的人，常会顺手牵羊，偷窃种种不怎样值钱的东西，通常是罐头之类物品。这是个心理上的问题，其根源是有迹可寻的。（《偷窃癖》，1992年1月17日《联合早报》《保健》版）

To Lead Away A Goat In Passing

This Chinese idiom means to conveniently walk off with someone else's property.

Example: "People who suffer from kleptomania tend to 'lead away a goat in passing'; they usually steal things of little value. This is a form of psycholopathic sickness." (Lianhe Zaobao 17/1/92)

顺水人情　shùnshuǐ rénqíng

顺水：船行驶的方向跟水流方向一致。指顺便做的人情：不费力而给人的好处。例如：柬埔寨反正需要外国派军队，派行政人员前来重建国家，公开邀请日本派"自卫队"到柬埔寨，不仅是做个顺水人情，还可投其所好，给日本自民党政府帮个忙。（《云生要求日本派兵》，1992年3月27日《联合早报》第14版）

A Favour Done In Passing

This Chinese idiom literally reads as "A favour done like following the stream", meaning the favour is done at little cost.

Example: "Since Cambodia needs to have the assistance of foreign troops and administrators in rebuilding its country, the open invitation for Japan to send its self-defence corps to Cambodia was not only 'a favour done in passing' but also a move made to the host's liking. It would be useful to the LDP government." (Lianhe Zaobao 27/3/92)

死皮赖脸 sǐ pí lài liǎn

　　形容厚着脸皮，继续胡搅、纠缠。例如：面对当前的俄罗斯局面，摆在耶尔辛面前只有三条路：……第二条路就是继续死皮赖脸地撑下去，把他那套按照常理是不可能行得通的激进经济改革政策"贯彻始终"。（《耶尔辛前途堪虑》，1992年1月29日《联合早报》第14版）

To Be Brazen-Faced

　　This Chinese idiom describes someone who is thick-skinned and hard to shake off.

　　Example: "One of the ways out for Yeltsin in the current Russian economic situation is 'to be brazen-faced' and persist in carrying out his seemingly impractical reforms." (Lianhe Zaobao 29/1/92)

添油加醋　tiān yóu jiā cù

　　比喻夸大事实，或在叙述事情经过时编造原来没有的内容或情节。例如：现在我（刘晓庆）看到或听到谣言，还会和朋友们评价这些谣言的水平，评出一、二、三名。有时候，还会和大家一起添油加醋，将这些故事加以发展，从中甚至会得到一些无可奈何的快乐。（《我为什么再写自传》，1992年5月1日《联合早报》《茶馆》版）

　　也说"加油添醋"或"添枝加叶"。

To Add Oil And Vinegar

This idiom means to exaggerate; to add colour, emphasis or details, even factitious ones to a narration.

Example: "Now, when I (the film star Liu Xiaoqing) hear or read a rumour about myself, I can even talk about it with friends. We will assess and grade its absurdity. We will 'add oil and vinegar' to develop the story, just to get some fun out of it." (Lianhe Zaobao 1/5/92)

甜言蜜语 *tián yán mì yǔ*

蜜糖一样的话。指为了讨人喜欢或哄骗（**hǒngpiàn**）人而说的话。例如：吴作栋总理说："如果我觉得事情应这么做，我会公开我的想法。我本来可以用甜言蜜语，但这不是我的个性。我是个有话直说的人，虽然有时这不是明智的做法，不过我宁可对自己忠实和对人民忠实。"（《把组屋翻新与选票挂钩，吴总理否认"威胁"选民》，1992年4月21日《联合早报》封面版）

也说成甜言美语/甘言美语/甜嘴蜜舌。

Sweet Words And Honeyed Phrases

This idiom often refers to fine-sounding words one uses to trick or hoodwink others.

Example: "PM Goh said, 'If I think things should be done this way, I will say so openly. I could have mouthed 'sweet words and honeyed phrases', but that's not me. I say what I think even if some poeple say it is unwise.' Mr Goh stressed that he would rather be honest to himself and the people." (Lianhe Zaobao 21/4/92)

铤而走险 tǐng ér zǒuxiǎn

铤：快跑的样子；走险：进行冒险活动。形容无路可走而采取冒险行动。例如：沙波什尼科夫当初支持耶尔辛的一个主要条件，是原苏联军队能在独联中继续保持统一。如今形势变了，沙波什尼科夫很难对独联军方领导层交代，独联军方铤而走险以捍卫自身地位的可能性并不能排除。（《独联军队前途难卜》，1992年3月19日《联合早报》社论）

"铤"也写成"挺"。

To Risk Danger In A Hasty Move

This Chinese idiom is mostly used to describe the reckless moves one is forced to take in desperation.

Example: "The main consideration for Marshal Yevgeni Shaposhnikov to support Boris Yeltsin was that the armed forces of the former Soviet Union should remain intact in the Commonwealth of Independent States. Now the situation has changed. Marshal Shaposhnikov will find it difficult to explain the state of affairs to the military leadership of CIS. The possibility of 'a reckless move in desperation' taken by The CIS military leaders in self-defence cannot be ruled out." (Lianhe Zaobao 19/3/92)

推陈出新　tuī chén chū xīn

指除去旧的，使它以新的面貌出现。例如：每一种产品都
有生命周期，必定要经过诞生、成长、成熟、衰亡四个阶段。
市场行销专家能做的是不断推陈出新，以新产品取代旧产品，
使产品生命得以延续。（《传统中药走向现代化》，1992年1
月31日《联合早报》第27版）

Weed Through The Old To Bring Forth The New

This Chinese idiom stresses the evolution of new things or ideas
out of the old.

Example: "Every product has a life cycle. It has to go through
the process of development, growth, maturity and decline.
Marketing specialists have to 'weed through the old to bring forth
the new', so as to extend the life of a product." (Lianhe Zaobao 31/
1/92)

脱胎换骨 tuō tāi huàn gǔ

　　道教的修炼者认为，如果得道，就脱凡胎而成圣胎，换凡骨而成仙骨。比喻通过教育和改造，根本改变一个人的立场和世界观。也指事物的彻底变化。例如：为了重整上海市经济和贸易中心的地位，上海市政府决定今年在南京路上兴建和改建十大项目。曾是上海最华丽、规模最大的大光明电影院也要脱胎换骨。（《上海南京路将换新貌》，1992年5月4日《联合早报》第16版）这个例句用的是上边第二个意思。

　　也说"换骨脱胎"。

To Be Recreated

This proverb literally reads, 'To cast off one's body grown from the foetus, and change one's mortal bones into immortal ones'. It is what the Taoists believe will happen when one achieves immortality through practising Taoism. It is now used to mean 'To thoroughly remould oneself or 'A complete change'.

Example: "In the plan to regain Shanghai's status as a trade and economic centre, the City Administration has decided to implement ten development and redevelopment projects at Nanjing Road. The largest cinema in Shanghai will also have 'to be recreated'." (Lianhe Zaobao 4/5/92)

挖空心思 wā kōng xīnsī

　　形容费尽心机，想尽办法。例如：目前德国的经济正走在
十字路口，各政党都在挖空心思，想用新的办法来拯救即将走
下坡的德国经济。虽然它目前还没有出现危机，但如果不早日
想出办法来，其前途可虑！（《德国经济出现衰退现象》，
1992年3月2日《联合早报》第13版）

To Rack One's Brains

This Chinese idiom means to crack one's head or put in great
effort to find a solution.

Example: "Presently, the German economy is at a crossroad. All
the political parties are 'racking their brains' to find a way to arrest
the declining trends. Although no crisis is yet in sight, the future
may be at stake if no solution is found soon." (Lianhe Zaobao 2/3/92)

歪打正着 wāi dǎ zhèng zháo

歪打下去，却正好打准。比喻方法本来不对头，却侥幸得到满意的结果。例如：提出"新思维"的戈尔巴乔夫，不仅是苏联的直接掘墓人，也间接的埋葬了美国……这一切，可以说是"戈思维"在发挥着歪打正着的作用——恐怕连戈尔巴乔夫自己都意料不到。（《"戈思维"歪打正着》，1992年1月1日《联合早报》第14版）

Hit A Mark By A Fluke

This Chinese idiom means to score a lucky hit.

Example: "By practising his 'new thinking', Gorbachev has not only dugged the grave for the Soviet Union, but also indirectly buried the US. He has really 'hit the mark by a fluke'." (Lianhe Zaobao 1/1/92)

外强中干 wài qiáng zhōng gān

原来是形容马外表看起来很强壮，但到作战时一紧张，显得很虚弱。现在形容人或事物外表上好像很强，实际上很弱。例如：老戈所说的苏联人民生活水准越来越追不上西方工业国，这种趋势在布列兹涅夫时代便开始明显化，事实上，亚洲的新兴工业经济体也远远的把苏联抛在后头。苏联早已是个外强中干的"超级强国"，强而不富，苏联迟早要走上衰亡的道路。（《不以成败论英雄》，1991年12月29日《联合早报》第2版）

Outwardly Strong But Inwardly Weak

This Chinese idiom is a sarcastic remark deriding one who looks impressive in appearance but lacks inner strength.

Example: "Gorbachev says the Soviet Union has lagged far behind Western industrialised countries. As a matter of fact, it has even fallen far behind Asia's Newly-Industrialised Economies. It is merely a 'outwardly strong but inwardly weak' superpower." (Lianhe Zaobao 29/12/1991)

亡羊补牢 *wáng yáng bǔ láo*

亡：丢失；牢：关牲口的圈。羊跑掉了，再去修补羊圈。比喻出了差错，要及时补救，免得再受损失。例如：警察总长韩聂夫昨日披露，警方将全面彻查梳邦机场失火事件，找出起火的原因，亡羊补牢，确保此事不会重演。（《警方将彻查梳邦机场失火原因，确保事件不再重演》，1992年4月12日《联合早报》第11版）

To Mend The Fold After A Sheep Is Lost

This is the first part of a Chinese old saying which means it will never be too late to correct a mistake.

Example: "The Chief of Police said there would be a full investigation into the fire at Subang Airport. 'To mend the fold after a sheep is lost' is to ensure that such incidents will not happen again." (Lianhe Zaobao 12/4/92)

望梅止渴 wàng méi zhǐ kě

　　曹操带领军队走到一个没有水的地方，兵士们渴得很。曹操骗他们说：前面有梅树林，到那里摘梅子吃，可以解渴。兵士听说有梅子可吃，口里都生出了口水，也就不那么渴了。比喻用空想或空话来安慰自己或别人。例如：劳工部准备为零售商店放宽雇用客工的条例，让只雇用两名本地雇员的商店也能雇用一名客工……但是，组屋商店有很多是连一名本地员工也请不到的商店，条例的放松也如同"望梅止渴"。（《中小型零售业今后的方向》，1992年3月4日《联合早报》第10版）

Quench One's Thirst By Thinking Of Plums

In the Tale of Three Kingdoms, Cao Cao once marched his army into a barren land. The soldiers were tormented by thirst. Cao deceived them by saying that there was a plum grove only a short distance ahead. The thought of tasting the plums made the soldiers slobber. They were not thirsty anymore. Hence this Chinese proverb means to console oneself with false hopes.

Example: "If the Ministry of Labour is to relax the restriction on employing foreign workers, it will allow the shopkeepers who are employing only two local employees to employ one foreign worker. But to many shopkeepers in HDB estates who cannot get even one local employee, the relaxing of restriction will only be 'quenching the thirst by thinking of plums'." (Lianhe Zaobao 4/3/92)

稳如泰山　wěn rú Tàishān

　　像泰山一样安稳，不可动摇。形容十分稳固。例如：今天是波斯湾战争开战的一周年纪念日，而头号战犯伊拉克总统胡申目前仍然稳如泰山。这场战争是不是结束得太早了呢？《新闻周刊》在一篇专题报道里揭露了当时白宫作出仓促停战决定的一些背景。（《波斯湾战争太早结束？》，1992年1月17日《联合早报》第32版）

　　"稳如"也说"安如"或"安若"。

As Stable As Mount Taishan

　　Mount Taishan is one of the highest mountains in China. This Chinese idiom uses its enormity to describe something that is firm and unshakable.

　　Example: "Today is the first anniversary of the Gulf War, yet the leading war criminal, President Saddam Hussein's position is still 'as stable as Mount Taishan'. The Newsweek revealed some details about how the White House had hastily decided to end the war." (Lianhe Zaobao 17/1/92)

无风不起浪　wú fēng bù qǐ làng

没有风就不会掀起波浪。比喻事情发生总有原因。例如：尽管我们目前还无法确定赵紫阳是否已获平反，却可以根据上述推理，得出中共高层无意处置赵紫阳的结论。问题只在于，他几时才能东山再起。

相信这个日子即将到来——毕竟，无风不起浪。（《阴霾（yīnmái）突消散，紫阳料重光》，1992年1月24日《联合早报》第29版）

There Are No Waves Without Wind

This Chinese proverb's English equivalent is "There is no smoke without fire."

Example: "Although we are unable to determine whether Zhao Ziyang's name has been cleared, it is reasonable to conclude that the Chinese Communist Party has no intention of punishing him. The question now is when he will make a comeback. We are sure that it would be soon, after all, 'there are no waves without wind'." (Lianhe Zaobao 24/1/92)

无孔不入　wú kǒng bù rù

　　孔：小洞。比喻利用一切机会进行活动。多指干坏事，含有贬义。例如：苏联这个在20世纪势力无孔不入的庞大帝国，是在不费一枪一弹的情况下和平瓦解，如今世界有安全感，有谁能不暗自喝采？有谁不惊叹一声"好一个戈尔巴乔夫"？（《不以成败论英雄》，1991年12月29日《联合早报》第2版）

　　"不入"也说"不钻"。

Taking Advantage Of Every Opportunity

　　Literally, this Chinese idiom describes something which pervades every opening. It is used figuratively to criticise a person who seizes every opportunity to do evil.

　　Example: "The Soviet Union was an empire in the 20th century which 'took advantage of every opportunity' to expand its influence. But it has now disintegrated without a single bullet being fired." (Lianhe Zaobao 29/12/91)

五十步笑百步　wǔ shí bù xiào bǎi bù

作战时，兵士逃跑，往后退了五十步的人讥笑退了一百步的人。比喻自己跟别人有同样的缺点或错误，只是程度不同罢了。例如：在笑话中国人不文明的自由餐抢吃镜头之余，忘记了我们在免费场合的表现，也不过是五十步笑百步。（《急待提升的国民素质》，1992年3月12日《联合早报》第16版）

One Who Retreats Fifty Paces Mocks One Who Retreats A Hundred

This idiom's English equivalence is 'the pot calls the kettle black'.

Example: "Those who ridicule the uncivil behaviour of the Chinese people scrambling for food at buffet lunches seem to forget their own behaviour at places where things are given free. This is exactly the case of 'one who retreats fifty paces mocks one who retreats a hundred'." (Lianhe Zaobao 12/3/92)

喜出望外 xǐ chū wàng wài

喜：喜悦；望外：希望或意料之外。出乎意料地高兴，多指遇到出乎意外的好事儿而高兴。例如：澳洲一名医生在家门口升美国国旗，正好给早上起来跑步的布斯看到。布斯回到旅馆就打电话给这名医生，邀请他和妻子到旅馆谈天，使他们喜出望外。（《在家门外升美国国旗，澳医生受邀会布斯》，1992年1月2日《联合早报》第19版）

To Be Pleasantly Surprised

This Chinese idiom is commonly used to describe the feeling of joy at an unexpected gain.

Example: "An Australian doctor was raising the US flag when President Bush jogged past his house. The President later called to invite him and his wife to the hotel for a chit chat. The doctor was 'pleasantly surprised'." (Lianhe Zaobao 2/1/92)

相辅相成　xiāng fǔ xiāng chéng

辅：辅助。两件事互相配合、辅助，互相促成。例如：中国的政治稳定和经济发展，给东南亚国家提供了许多机会；而相应地，东南亚华人经济圈的力量，也可对中国的经济建设，起着相辅相成的作用。（《成功的外交姿态》，1992年1月11日《联合早报》社论）

也说"相辅而成"。

To Complement Each Other

This Chinese idiom means to supplement each other or to help each other.

Example: "Political stability and economic development in China offer countries in South-east Asia many opportunities; similarly, the economic strength of the overseas Chinese in the region also helps China to develop its economy. They actually 'complement each other'." (Lianhe Zaobao 11/1/92)

小心翼翼　xiǎoxīn yìyì

　　翼翼：恭敬的样子。原来形容恭敬、严肃的样子。后来形容十分谨慎，一点儿不敢疏忽。例如：吴作栋总理在五一劳动节献词中说，在目前捉摸不定的形势下，我们应该格外小心，不要让成本，特别是工资成本，达到我们不能维持的水平。我们宁可小心翼翼，避免基薪增加幅度太大。（《吴总理劝请国人，经济增长虽较慢，不必过度惊慌》，1992年5月1日《联合早报》封面版）

To Be Doubly Cautious

　　The second part of this Chinese idiom is an adverbial phrase which originally means 'respectfully' and 'seriously'. Now it is used more often to mean 'prudently'.

　　Example: "PM Goh in his May Day message says we should 'be doubly cautious' in order not to allow costs, especially wage costs, to go up to unsustainable levels in the face of an uncertain economic situation." (Lianhe Zaobao 1/5/92)

笑容可掬 xiàoróng kě jū

笑容：含笑的神情；掬：两手捧起来。形容满脸堆笑的样子。例如：笑容可掬的美国第一夫人芭芭拉布斯，昨天参观东京一家百货公司的美国货品，说她希望日本人多多购买美国货。（《布斯夫人逛百货公司》，1992年1月9日《联合早报》第32版）

To Be Radiant With Smiles

This Chinese idiom describes someone who is all smiles.

Example: "US First Lady, Barbara Bush, who was 'radiant with smiles', went to department stores in Tokyo to look at American goods on display. She hopes more Japanese would buy US products." (Lianhe Zaobao 9/1/92)

心照不宣 xīnzhào bù xuān

心照：不必对方明说，心中自然明白。不宣：不必明说。彼此心里明白，用不着说出来。例如：尽管日本已经完全具备了从军事上保护自己的经济实力，但是日本的邻国都不愿意看到日本重新成为军事大国，因此无论北京、台北还是汉城、平壤，乃至马尼拉、新加坡，东亚各国都心照不宣地希望美国继续"保护"日本。（《日本还不能说"不"》，1992年1月9日《联合早报》第19版）

To Share A Tacit Understanding

This Chinese idiom describes those who share a common feeling or mutual understanding but without having to express it openly.

Example: "Although Japan has the economic capability to protect itself militarily, its neighbours do not want it to become a military power once more. Whether it be Beijing, Taipei, Seoul or Pyongyang, or even Manila or Singapore, all the East Asian countries 'share a tacit understanding': they want US to continue 'protecting' Japan." (Lianhe Zaobao 9/1/92)

兴师问罪 xīng shī wèn zuì

兴师：起兵；问罪：宣布对方的罪状而加以讨伐。本指宣布罪状，发兵讨伐。现多用来指严厉责问。例如：案发时死者失业，因为不满女友移情别恋，才带朋友一齐兴师问罪，想不到因双方激烈争吵而导致冲突，惹来杀身之祸。（《失业汉被判死刑》，1992年1月10日《联合早报》第5版。杀身之祸：shā shēn zhī huò，成语，自身遭杀害的大祸。）

To Send A Punitive Expedition Against (Someone)

"Xing shi" means to send an army; "wen zui" means to denounce. This Chinese idiom commonly describes an action to denounce someone publicly for his crimes or serious errors.

Example: "Earlier, the deceased was unhappy that his girl friend had deserted him and wanted to 'send a punitive expedition against' her. But the ensuing quarrel ended up in a fight that led to his death." (Lianhe Zaobao 10/1/92)

袖手旁观 xiù shǒu páng guān

袖手：把手笼（lóng）在袖筒里。把手笼在袖筒里，站在一旁观看。形容对事情一点也不关心，既不过问，也不协助。
例如：事实上足总为国家队的初选球员都买了保险，同时还有一笔为照顾球员福利而设的基金。如果国家队初选球员在训练时受了伤，足总绝不会袖手旁观的，（《足总已拟定迈克瓦纳薪酬》，1992年3月13日《联合早报》）

Look On With Hands Folded In The Sleeves

This Chinese proverb means to keep oneself away from involvement.

Examples: "The Football Association of Singapore has bought insurance for every player from the very first round of selection. There is also a special fund which will be used for players' welfare. FAS will never 'look on with hands folded in the sleeves' should any national player suffer any injury." (Lianhe Zaobao 13/3/92)

雪上加霜　xuě shàng jiā shuāng

比喻灾难或祸患接着发生，使受害程度加深。例如：1969年3月珍宝岛冲突之后，毛泽东在中共中央文革碰头会上作出了国际形势可能恶化的判断。为了对付苏联"社会帝国主义"的军事威胁，毛泽东发出了"要准备打仗"、"备战、备荒、为人民"、"深挖洞、广积粮、不称霸"等一系列"最高指示"，几乎使整个中国变成了一座大军营，本来已因文革大受影响的中国经济因此而雪上加霜。（《"共产帝国主义"与"社会帝国主义"》，1992年2月16日《联合早报》第2版）

To Add Frost To Snow

This Chinese idiom describes figuratively the occurence of one disaster after another.

Example: "After China's border clash with the Soviet Union, Mao Zedong predicted a situation that will worsen and ordered the people to get fully prepared. The high-level directive almost turned the whole country into an army camp. It was like 'adding frost to snow' as the economy had already been badly wrecked by the Cultural Revolution." (Lianhe Zaobao 16/2/92)

揠苗助长 yà miáo zhù zhǎng

揠：拔。中国古代宋国有个人，嫌禾苗长得慢，就一棵棵地把禾苗往上拔起一点，回家还夸口说："今天我帮助苗长了！"他儿子听了赶忙到田里去看，苗都枯死了。比喻急于求成，反而坏事。例如：在不同年龄的分界上，以适合高年级的智商题目来测验低年级的学生，是揠苗助长式的作法，对儿童的智力发展未必有益。（《揠苗助长，弊多于利》，1992年3月28日，《联合早报》的第14版）

也说"拔苗助长"。

Pulling The Shoots To Help Them Grow

A man in the ancient kingdom of Song was not happy with the slow growth of the rice shoots. He decided to help by pulling all the shoots upward a little bit. He went home and bragged about it. On hearing this his son rushed to the field to have a look. The rice shoots were all withering. Thus, this Chinese proverb means 'Impatience can only be counter-productive'.

Example: "On the division of age-grades, the use of assessment papers designed for students of a higher IQ for testing those at a lower level is 'pulling the shoots to help them grow'. This may not prove productive." (Lianhe Zaobao 28/3/92)

一干二净 yī gān èr jìng

　　形容一点儿也不剩。例如：职总认为，雇主给人的印象是，他们已对工友在八十年代中期经济衰退时，接受削减15%的公积金缴交率所作的牺牲，忘得一干二净。（《职总要求雇主全面恢复公积金缴交率》，1992年1月21日《联合早报》第5版）

To Be Absolutely Complete Or Thorough

　　This Chinese idiom literally means to do something very thoroughly.

　　Example: "NTUC feels that employers seem to have forgotten 'completely' the sacrifice made by the workers when they accepted the 15% cut in CPF contribution during the economic recession in the mid 1980s." (Lianhe Zaobao 21/1/92)

一叶知秋　yī yè zhī qiū

看到一片落叶，就知道秋天要来了。比喻从某些细微的迹象，可以预料到事物的变化和发展的趋向。例如：美国经济振兴乏力，联邦储备局主席格林斯潘说，严峻程度是他有生以来所仅见，世界最大公司通用汽车大量关厂裁员更是一叶知秋。（《布斯亚太之行一箭双雕》，1991年12月31日《联合早报》第10版）

也说成"叶落知秋"。

The Fall Of One Leaf Heralds The Autumn

This Chinese idiom's English equivalent is "It's a straw in the wind." It means a small sign can indicate a great trend.

Example: "The US economy is in the doldrums and the chairman of the Federal Reserve Board said it is the worst he has ever seen. The retrenchment at GM, the world's largest car maker also indicates that 'the fall of the leaf heralds the autumn'." (Lianhe Zaobao 31/12/91)

以身作则 yǐ shēn zuò zé

则：表率（biǎoshuài）、榜样。用自身的行动做出榜样。例如：世界著名影星阿诺·苏施内格（A r n o l d Schwarzenegger）认为，要鼓励孩子健身，家长必须以身作则，他们应少看一点电视，每天抽出时间，带着孩子一块儿去运动。（《著名影星阿诺强调，孩子保健父母有责》，1992年5月1日《联合早报》的12版）

To Set A Standard With One's Own Deeds

This proverb stresses the point that deeds are more persuasive than words.

Example: "The world-famous film star Arnold Schwarzenegger thinks that to encourage children to keep fit, parents have 'to set an example'. They should cut down TV watching and spend more time exercising with their children." (Lianhe Zaobao 1/5/92)

应接不暇　yìngjiē bù xiá

　　不暇：没有空闲，忙不过来。形容来人或事情太多，应付不过来。例如：中国国内和海外的游客近来纷纷涌向长江，赶着去游览三峡，使中国的旅游航运部门应接不暇。（《长江三峡旅游热，前年掀起，今春更旺》，1992年4月14日《联合早报》第13版）

More Than One Can Cope With

This proverb means one is no longer able to cope with the influx of work.

Example: "Recently, local and foreign tourists in China have been rushing to the upper reaches of Changjiang (Yangtze River) to visit the Three Gorges. This has given the tourism and transport sectors 'more work than they can cope with'." (Lianhe Zaobao 14/4/92)

油尽灯枯　yóu jìn dēng kū

尽：用完；枯：水分全没有了。油灯里的油用完了，灯也就成了一盏（zhǎn）枯灯。比喻力气用完或生命到了尽头。例如：我们不能只看到西方消费文明的灯火辉煌，对它逐渐油尽灯枯的另一方面却视而不见。（《两次抽样调查的结果》，1992年2月25日《联合早报》社论）

有条俗语叫"油干灯草尽"或"油尽捻子（niǎnzi，油灯的灯芯）干"，跟"油尽灯枯"同义。

The Lamp Extinguishes When The Oil Runs Out

This Chinese idiom figuratively describes the end of a human life or a system when the sustaining energy or activating forces have exhausted.

Example: "We should not keep on admiring the prosperity of Western consumerism without realising that 'the lamp will extinguish when the oil runs out'." (Lianhe Zaobao 25/2/92)

雨后春笋　yǔ hòu chūnsǔn

春笋：春天长成或挖出来的各种竹笋。春天下过雨之后，竹笋长得又多又快。比喻事物大量涌现并蓬勃发展。例如：越南具有庞大的发展潜能，可能成为一个新兴的市场，所以越来越吸引投资者注意。而在政府允许国内进行西方式的经济改革之后，越南全国各地的小商家已如雨后春笋般林立，当局还有计划在胡志明市建立第一个经济特区。（《越南发奋图强》，1992年1月4日《联合早报》第15版）

Spring Up Like Bamboo Shoots

This Chinese idiom uses the spontaneous sprouting of bamboo shoots after a spring rain to describe the simultaneous growth or emergence of something.

Example: "Vietnam has great development potential and is attractive to foreign investors. Since the government implemented economic reforms, many small businesses have 'sprung up like bamboo shoots' all over the country." (Lianhe Zaobao 4/1/92)

怨声载道 yuàn shēng zài dào

怨声：怨恨的声音；载：充满。怨恨的声音充满道路。形容人民普遍愤恨，强烈不满。例如：前苏联的经济虽然一团糟，可是新的经济改革计划并不见得比过去好。目前物价飞涨，俄罗斯人怨声载道。许多地区已爆发群众示威事件，抗议总统耶尔辛的市场导向经济改革计划。（《俄罗斯国会议长说，政府非常无能，应该辞职》，1992年1月14日《联合早报》封面版）

"载道" 也说 "满路"。

Cries of Discontent Are Heard Everywhere

This Chinese idiom is commonly used to describe widespread and strong feelings of dissatisfaction among the people over certain issues.

Example: "Although the Soviet economy in the past was in a mess, it is even worse now. With skyrocketing prices of goods, 'cries of discontent are heard everywhere'. There were demonstrations to protest against Yeltsin's market reforms." (Lianhe Zaobao 14/1/92)

斩钉截铁　zhǎn dīng jié tiě

　　比喻说话、办事果断、坚决，毫不犹豫。例如：秀卿说，她买衣服主要是看款式和手工，价钱倒是其次，遇上合心意的，她通常很舍得花钱。

　　"我花了会有一点点心痛，但不后悔。"她斩钉截铁地说。（《姐儿爱靓妆，口袋钱花光》，1992年1月9日《联合早报》《影艺》版）

　　也可以倒过来说成"截铁斩钉"。

Absolute And Decisive

Literally, this Chinese idiom means to act like cutting nails and breaking iron. It figuratively describes one who speaks or behaves with decisiveness or curt finality.

Examples: "Xiu Qing said that when she went shopping for dresses, she always looked for the fashion rather than good bargain. If she liked the design, she would buy without any regret. She said it in an 'absolute and decisive' manner." (Lianhe Zaobao 9/1/92)

张冠李戴 Zhāng guān Lǐ dài

冠：帽子。把姓张的人的帽子戴到姓李的头上。比喻弄错了对象或事实。例如：一名读者最近写信向本报指出，"新加坡今昔展览会"上的部分展品出现"张冠李戴"的现象，照片与说明中地点不符。（《新加坡今昔展览部分照片弄错》，1992年4月22日《联合早报》第4版）

To Put Zhang's Hat On Li's Head

This idiom means 'to confuse one with another'.

Example: "A reader writes in to point out that there were cases of 'putting Zhang's hat on Li's head' in the recent Singapore Now and Then Photo Exhibition. The places referred to in the captions for some of the pictures were not those shown in the pictures." (Lianhe Zaobao 22/4/90)

招兵买马　zhāo bīng mǎi mǎ

招兵：招募人来当兵；买马：购买战马。原本形容组织或扩充武装力量。比喻组织或扩充人力。例如：陈迹说："其实早在80年代初，处在萌芽阶段的新广戏剧组正在招兵买马，我和黄文永及柯莎菲一样，都曾经来新加坡投考，后来由于客观原因，我无法像他们那样加入新广。"（《陈迹一生为戏忙》，1992年1月29日《联合早报》《影艺》版）

"招兵"也说"招军"，也可以倒过来说成"买马招兵（军）"。

To Recruit Men And Buy Horses

This Chinese idiom means to expand the strength of the army by enlisting more people and horses. It is now more often used to describe measures to enlarge the manpower of a company.

Example: "Chen Ji said when SBC's Drama Section started 'to recruit men and horses' in the early 80s, he was among the first to apply. But circumstances prevented him from joining." (Lianhe Zaobao 29/1/92)

争先恐后 zhēng xiān kǒng hòu

只怕落后而抢着往前。例如：25岁的沙善说："他们没有东西可以取暖，不得不乱砍白杨树和松树。"

为了取得燃料，阿尔巴尼亚人争先恐后伐木，结果是：从首都到都拉斯港的公路两旁的树木，全消失了；卡瓦亚镇的两座小森林，不见了。（《阿尔巴尼亚人民砍街树当燃料》，1992年1月17日《联合早报》第31版）

也可以倒过来说成"恐后争先"。

Rushing To Be Ahead Of Others

Literally, this Chinese idiom means to strive to be the first and be afraid of lagging behind. It is used to describe people who vie with each other frantically to achieve personal gains.

Example: "The shortage of fuel in Albania has resulted in people 'rushing to be ahead of others' in cutting down the trees that line the road. Many trees, including those in two small woodlands have totally disappeared." (Lianhe Zaobao 17/1/92)

众矢之的 zhòng shǐ zhī dì

众：许多；矢：箭；的：箭靶的中心。许多支箭所射的靶子，比喻很多人攻击的目标。例如：一些分析家认为，耶尔辛因为没有什么建树，戈尔巴乔夫这棵大树被锯去之后，耶尔辛将会是众矢之的，这是肯定的。他想在今后能够保持他的皇座，首先需以最短的时间把经济搞好，但可能性极小，西方再用多少钱来填补也无济于事。（《克里姆林宫出了新沙皇》，1991年12月27日《联合早报》第15版。无济于事：wú jì yú shì，对事情没有帮助。）

The Target Of Public Criticisms

Literally, this Chinese idiom means the target of many arrows. It is used to describe a person who has incurred public wrath.

Example: "Some analysts believe that after the removal of Gorbachev, Yeltsin will become 'the target of public criticisms' as he has not achieved anything. To preserve his position, he has to improve the economy, but his chances of success are slim. " (Lianhe Zaobao 27/12/91)

自圆其说　zì yuán qí shuō

圆：圆满、完整。把自己的说法表达得周全圆满，没有一点漏洞。例如：金日成将朝鲜河山视为私产，最高统治权父传子，家天下，这在东方的政治生活中并不少见，金日成也可在国内自圆其说。（《金日成父子的"只开放不改革"》，1992年5月4日《联合早报》第13版）

也说"自完其说"，完：完全、完满。

To Make One's Own Statement Plausible

This proverb at times also means 'to justify oneself'.

Example: "Kim II Song sees North Korea as his private property, and the supreme ruling power a family legacy which he can hand down to his son and later his son to his son's son and so on. In fact, this is not uncommon in the oriental political style. Kim can indeed 'make his statement plausible' in his own country." (Lianhe Zaobao 4/5/92)

走马上任　zǒu mǎ shàng rèn

走马：骑马奔驰。指官员就职，现也指去担当某项工作。例如：卫奕信四年前走马上任，接替在北京访问时病逝的前港督尤德。无论卫奕信、尤德，又或者再前一任的麦理浩，都是由英国外交部委派到香港出任总督一职的。（《港督换人无碍政经发展》，1992年1月3日《联合早报》社论）

"上任"也说"赴任"或"到任"。

To Assume Official Duty

Government officials in olden China rode on horse back to take up their new postings usually in places far away from home. This Chinese idiom has now come to mean anyone who starts on a new job.

Example: "Sir David Wilson 'assumed official duty' following the death of the former HK governor four years ago. All HK governors in the past had been appointed by the British Foreign Office." (Lianhe Zaobao 3/1/91)

左右为难 zuǒyòu wéinán

左右：左和右两方面；为难：感到不好应付。形容不管怎么做都有难处。例如：两年前北京发生六四事件，导致中英关系陷入另一场低潮。这次突发事件，也使身处夹缝中的卫奕信左右为难。（《港督换人无碍政经发展》，1992年1月3日《联合早报》社论）

"为难"也说"两难"。

To Be In An Awkward Predicament

Literally, this Chinese idiom means to find difficulties in moving in both the left and right directions. It describes one who is in a dilemma.

Example: "The Tiananmen Square incident two years ago greatly strained diplomatic relations between China and Britain. It also placed Sir David Wilson 'in an awkward predicament'." (Lianhe Zaobao 3/1/91)

帮亲不帮理　bāng qīn bù bāng lǐ

这条俗语是由"帮理不帮亲"变化而来，二者意思相反。"帮理不帮亲"的意思是：帮人说话，要被帮的人有理，如果无理，即使是至亲好友也不能相帮。"帮亲不帮理"意思正好相反。例如：身为中正的一分子，我们不能让"爱校"冲昏了头，而"帮亲不帮理"。我批评学校，是希望现今与未来的中正全体老师能够在更舒服、现代化的设备下培育栋梁，为社会，为国家做一番贡献。

（《批评就意味着不爱校吗？》，1992年1月28日《联合早报》第14版）

To Side With The Kin Rather Than The Right

This Chinese proverb is the exact opposite of "to side with the right rather than the kin". It criticises one who supports someone just because he is a relative, although he is in the wrong.

Example: "Although I was a student of Chung Cheng High School, I would not 'side with the kin rather than the right'. My criticism of the school was done in the hope that all the teachers could educate their students in a more congenial environment in future." (Lianhe Zaobao 28/1/92)

大哥别说二哥，大家都差不多
dà gē bié shuō èr gē, dàjiā dōu chàbuduō

比喻有相同或类似情况的人不要互相挑剔指责。例如：在世界各国，当明星都一样，总是有许多的绯闻困扰，可是那些国家的观众注意力比较分散，谣言也分布得比较平均。今天是你杀了人，明天就是她生了私生子，后天又是另一个贩毒，等等等等。这样一来，明星们就会觉得无所谓，因为"大哥别说二哥，大家都差不多"。（《我为什么再写自传》，1992年5月1日《联合早报》《茶馆》版）

The Eldest Brother Does Not Find Fault With The Second Brother As Both Are About The Same

This common saying means 'Those who are in similar situations should not or do not reproach or counsel each other'.

Example: "Film stars everywhere are the same. They are bound to be affected by scandals. But in some countries there are more things to divert fans' attention. Assaults of rumours tend to scatter more evenly. Nevertheless, few film stars are spared. So one can take it lightly as 'the eldest brother does not find fault with the second as both are about the same'." (Lianhe Zaobao 1/5/92)

今朝有酒今朝醉　jīnzhāo yǒu jiǔ jīnzhāo zuì

今天有酒，喝醉了再说。比喻只求眼前享乐，不作长远打算。也指过一天算一天。例如：我国经济发展快，人们追求物质生活享受的需求也越来越大，对先透支后付款的诱惑不易抵挡。人们多带着"今朝有酒今朝醉"的享受人生想法，不只为自己申请信用卡，阔气的父母也为孩子申请附属卡。（《管制信用卡是明智做法》，1992年1月4日《联合早报》第14版）

"今朝"也说"今天"或"今夕"。

这条俗语后边还可以接一句：明日愁来明日愁/明日愁来明日当/明日乏钞又商量/莫管门前是与非。

To Let Tomorrow Take Care Of Itself

Literally, this Chinese proverb means if there is wine today, let's drink until we are drunk, tomorrow is another day. It is used to describe the easy lifestyle of those who are happy-go-lucky.

Example: "Our increasingly affluent society has made more people go for material enjoyment. Enjoy first and pay later seems to be an irresistible temptation. Many people are adopting the attitude of 'let tomorrow take care of itself....'" (Lianhe Zaobao 4/1/92)

敬酒不吃吃罚酒 jìng jiǔ bù chī chī fá jiǔ

敬酒：宴席上斟上酒，有礼貌地请人喝；罚酒：用喝酒来处罚别人。比喻好说不听，等到被逼或受惩罚时才去干。例如：这回，布斯到日本，料将施压要日本汽车公司增加采用美制组件，多输入美国木制品、白米和电脑，否则"敬酒不吃吃罚酒"，让民主党控制的国会两院通过贸易条例对付你。（《布斯亚太行一箭双雕》，1991年12月31日《联合早报》第10版）

"敬酒"也说"赏酒"。

Refuse A Toast Only To Drink A Forfeit

This Chinese proverb is used to describe a person who is constrained to do what he at first declined.

Example: "The visit by President Bush to Japan is to apply pressure on the country to import more car components and other US products. If Japan disagrees, it may be 'refusing a toast only to drink a forfeit' as the US Congress may resort to trade restriction measures." (Lianhe Zaobao 31/12/91)

马死落地行 mǎ sǐ luò dì xíng

马死了，骑马的人只好下来步行了。比喻失去了依靠。例如：今年初，苏联已大量减少对越南的经济援助和贷款，并取消种种贸易优惠。这一变化，对在经济上严重依赖苏联的越南，是沉重的打击。俗语说："马死落地行"。在这样的情况下，越南只好自力更生，设法和资本主义国家修好，同时探讨经济援助的新途径。（《越南发奋图强》，1992年1月4日《联合早报》第5版。奋发图强：fā fèn tú qiáng，成语，振作起来，谋求强盛。自力更生：zì lì gēngshēng，成语，靠自己的力量把事情做好。）

To Rely On The Last Resort

Literally, this Chinese proverb means when the horse dies, the rider has to get down and walk. It figuratively means one who has lost his sole dependence and has now to resort to the last course of action.

Example: "When the Soviet Union cut off all aid and preferential trade with Vietnam, it was a big blow to the Vietnamese economy. Now, it has 'to rely on the last resort' by improving its relations with the capitalist countries and to seek economic assistance." (Lianhe Zaobao 4/1/92)

满招损，谦受益 mǎn zhāo sǔn, qiān shòu yì

满：骄傲自满；谦：谦虚、虚心。骄傲自满会招来损失，谦虚可以得到益处。例如：无论赛前或赛后，无论冲击全国记录成功或失败，耀文都很乐意接受访问，做到有问必答，完全没有架子。俗语说："满招损，谦受益。"态度谦和的耀文必能取得更大的成绩。（《霍耀文对自己要求高》，1992年3月24日《联合早报》第20版）

One Loses By Pride And Gains By Modesty

This old Chinese saying is often used to exhort those who are successful not to be proud, smug or complacent.

Example: "At any time before or after a competition, and in any event where he had succeeded or failed to break a record, Huo Yao-wen would gladly oblige the press by answering questions in a unassuming manner. As the old saying goes, 'one loses by pride and gains by modesty', the modest and amiable young man will definitely achieve greater success in the future." (Lianhe Zaobao 24/3/92)

墙倒众人推 qiáng dǎo zhòngrén tuī

众人：大家。墙已经倒了，大家还要来推一把。比喻大家
都表示反对。例如：用墙倒众人推的方法鞭挞（biāntà，鞭
打，比喻抨（pēng）击）一个已经死亡的对象，这太容易了。
我认为我们应该从历史的角度来研究探讨，苏联这个活了70多
年的国家，怎么就这样轻易地死去。（《回顾苏联的兴与
亡》，《联合早报》1992年1月31日第19版）

这条俗语也比喻一个人一旦失势或遭殃，大家就趁机欺侮
他，打击他。这条俗语的前边或后边还可以加一句："破鼓乱
人捶"。捶：chuí，敲打。

Everybody Hits A Man Who Is Down

Literally, this Chinese proverb means when a wall is about to
collapse, everybody gives it a push. It figuratively describes an unani-
mous opposition to an unpopular measure.

Example: "It is extremely easy for 'everybody to hit a man who
is down'. I feel that we should study the matter with greater depth
from the historical point of view. How could a country like the
Soviet Union which existed for 70 over years suddenly collapse and
demise?" (Lianhe Zaobao 31/1/92)

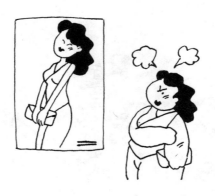

人比人，气死人 rén bǐ rén, qì sǐ rén

人和人相比，社会地位和生活条件往往相差很大，境况和遭遇差的，就会气得活不下去。指事事处处跟别人比较，只有自寻烦恼。例如：人们拿自己的际遇跟别人相比时，多半会发出不平之鸣，也许是"人比人气死人"吧。有的人不平于工作能力比他差的竟然做了他的上司；有的人不平于自己因老实而生意失败，别人因为会钻营走歪路而成功；好人没好报的事，更容易引起人们对老天爷不公平的同声谴责。（《确保人人有公平的起步》，1992年3月1日《联合早报》第2版）

也说"人比人，活不成"或"人比人，气煞（shà）人"。

By Comparing With Others, One Becomes Frustrated

The fortune and achievement of people in a society vary from person to person. Anyone who tries to compare himself with others is bound to be frustrated.

Example: "Many people tend to compare themselves with others. The result is a lot of unhappiness. This may be due to the fact that 'by comparing with others, one becomes frustrated'. Those who are not as successful as others always complain that they have not been treated fairly." (Lianhe Zaobao 1/3/92)

若要人不知，除非己莫为

ruò yào rén bù zhī, chúfēi jǐ mò wéi

若：如果；莫：不要；为：做。要想让人家不知道，除非自己不去干。通常是指做什么事，说什么话，是瞒不住人的。

例如："若要人不知，除非己莫为"。在日本正义人士的大力挖掘下，一些足以证明日本政府曾经策划拐带妇女充当"慰安妇"的史料先后公开了，使有关方面无法再厚着脸皮赖帐。（《日本热门话题——"慰安妇"》，1992年3月26日《联合早报》第17版）

If You Don't Want Others To Know About It, Don't Do It

This Chinese old saying simply means no one can hide his wrong doing.

Example: "As the old saying goes, 'if you don't want others to know about it, don't do it', and thanks to the great efforts of those righteous Japanese, historical data which bear testimony to the Japanese government's involvement in the evildoing of 'Comfor Women' have been unearthed. The authorities can no longer disavow it brazenly." (Lianhe Zaobao 26/3/92)

三个和尚挑水没水喝 sān gè héshang tiāo shuǐ méi shuǐ hē

一个和尚挑水，两个和尚抬水，三个和尚没水喝。比喻人一多，互相依赖扯皮，反而什么事也干不成。例如：

问：对外开放的过程中出现了些什么问题？

答：主要是官僚作风严重，机构重叠，办事效率很差。明明能办的事也要拖三推四，明明一个人能办的事，也要由三个人去做，正如中国人的老话："三个和尚挑水没水喝"。这令投资者感到很不方便，浪费他们的时间。我们正在设法纠正这些不良风气。（《符合产业政策的投资都受欢迎》，1992年1月8日《联合早报》第21版）

"喝"也说"吃"；"挑水"也可以省略。

Too Many Cooks Spoil The Broth

Literally, this Chinese proverb means that if three monks went to fetch water together, none of them have any to drink in the end. It satirizes those who passed the buck to others and accomplished nothing materially.

Example: "The inefficiency of Chinese business corporations is mainly because a job which can be done by one person is carried out by several people, in the end, 'too many cooks spoil the broth'. As a result, investors are inconvenienced. We are now trying to rectify the situation." (Lianhe Zaobao 8/1/92)

上梁不正下梁歪 shàngliáng bù zhèng xiàliáng wāi

梁：架在墙上或柱子上支撑房顶的横木；上梁：上边的梁。比喻上边的人行为不端正下边的人就跟着学坏。例如：江泽民还谈到廉政建设问题。他说，在经济搞上去的同时，要加强精神文明建设，做到拒腐蚀，永不沾……一方面要加强教育，另一方面要建立法制和健全规章制度。俗话说，上梁不正下梁歪。领导干部一定要做廉政建设的带头人，对贪污受贿的一定要严办。（《江泽民谈冲破思想束缚》，1992年3月29日《联合早报》第29版）

If The Upper Beam Is Not Straight The Lower One Will Go Slant

This Chinese saying means 'When those above behave unworthily, those below will do the same'.

Example: "Touching on the problem of corrupt practices, Mr Jiang Zemin said that when building up its economy, China would also maintain a clean and honest government. It would be done through greater effort in civic education and the establishment of the legal system together with rules and regulations. As the old saying goes, 'If the upper beam is not straight, the lower one will go slant', the leading officials must set a good example. Anyone who takes a bribe should be severely dealt with." (Lianhe Zaobao 29/3/92)

天塌下来当被盖 tiān tā xiàlai dàng bèi gài

当：作为；被：被子。比喻困难再大也不怕，自有办法解决。例如：安伦是四个弟弟和一个妹妹的大哥，从小就已经形成"天塌下来当被盖"的性格，不管多么陌生的东西，只要经过一段时间，就会适应。（《王安伦北京创新猷》，1992年1月27日《联合早报》《现代生活》版。新猷：xīnyóu，新的计划。）

这条俗语还有好几种说法，如：天塌了，还有撑天大汉哩/天塌下来屋顶着/天塌了有地接着/天塌下来有人顶等。

Let The Sky Be My Quilt Should It Fall On Me

This Chinese proverb means even if a horrendous disaster should strike, I will treat it as a blessed occurrence. It highlights the courage and adaptability of a person.

Example: "An Lun has four brothers and one sister. From a very young age, he has acquired a 'let the sky be my quilt should it fall on me' attitude. Therefore, whenever he is in a new surrounding, he adapts quickly." (Lianhe Zaobao 27/1/92)

天下没有不散的筵席 tiānxià méiyǒu bù sàn de yánxí

筵席：酒席。比喻有聚必有散，没有只聚不散的。也比喻一切事情都有一个结局。例如：长期以来，蒙古靠苏联的援助，然而天下没有不散的筵席。如今莫斯科都自己顾不过来，从1990年起中止了对包括蒙古在内的盟国的援助，并要求乌兰巴托偿还160亿美元的债款。（《蒙古市场经济前途坎坷》，坎坷kánkě，道路不平的样子。1992年2月18日《联合早报》第13版）

"没有"也说"无"，"不散"也说"百年不散"。也可以在前边加一句，说成"千里搭长棚，没个不散的筵席"。

All Parties Must Come To An End

This Chinese proverb stresses the fact that all happy occasions would not last forever.

Example: "For a long time, Mongolia had depended on the Soviet Union for aid. But 'all parties must come to an end'. Moscow, itself in grave trouble, has stopped all aid to its allies, including Mongolia, and is now asking for the repayment of debts amounting to US$16 billion." (Lianhe Zaobao 18/2/92)

为人不做亏心事，不怕夜半鬼敲门
wéirén bù zuò kuīxīn shì, bùpà yèbàn guǐ qiāo mén

为人：处世做人；亏心：自己觉得言论和行动违背正理；夜半：半夜。指平时没有做过违背良心的事，即使半夜三更有鬼来敲门，也用不着害怕。例如：既然以色列主动要求美国检查是否向中国出售爱国者导弹，自然是"为人不做亏心事，不怕夜半鬼敲门"。（《近乎奇谈的中以军火交易》，1992年3月18日《联合早报》第14版）

这条俗语还有好几种讲法，如：日间不作亏心事，半夜敲门不吃惊/平生不作亏心事，夜半敲门心不惊。

One Has No Fear When One Has A Clear Conscience

This Chinese saying literally reads as 'one who has done nothing against one's conscience will have no fear even if the ghost comes knocking at one's door in the middle of the night'.

Example: "Since Israel has, on its own initiative, asked the United States to carry out inspections to see whether it had sold the Patriot missile to China, it is clearly a case of 'one who has a clear conscience will have no fear even if the ghost knocks at one's door'." (Lianhe Zaobao 18/3/92)

稳坐钓鱼船 wěn zuò diào yú chuán

常跟"任凭风浪起"连用，指在大风大浪中沉着镇定，不慌不忙。比喻面对复杂的情况，仍然十分冷静沉着，毫不慌乱。例如：蔡志勇在1965年创立"曼克顿互惠基金"赚到大钱，然后把它卖给一家名叫CNA的大保险公司。第二年，"曼克顿互惠基金"的股价大跌，但蔡志勇已换回CNA的股份，他稳坐钓鱼船，丝毫未受损失。（《华人金融魔术师蔡志勇》，1992年2月19日《联合早报》第17版）。

"风浪起"也说"风浪险"或"风波险"；"钓鱼船"也说"钓鱼台"。

To Sit Firmly On A Fishing Boat

It means to remain calm and unruffled despite the tumultuous storm.

Example: "Cai Zhiyong set up the Manhattan Fund in 1965 which was very profitable. However, after he sold it to CNA, its shares began to plunge. But by then Cai was already holding CNA shares and was able 'to sit firmly on a fishing boat' and remained unscathed." (Lianhe Zaobao 19/2/91)

相骂没好言，相打没好拳

xiāng mà méi hǎo yán, xiāng dǎ méi hǎo quán

在对骂或打架时，由于感情冲动，双方往往不顾一切，言语行动失去约束。指人在吵架时态度就不会好。例如：飞达旅行社（马）有限公司总经理刘肇滋昨天看了有关报道说，新马原是一家人，人民世代友好，不应为了技术上的问题而斗气。他认为，"相骂没好言，相打没好拳"，大家应该冷静下来。（《新山中华商会会长刘南辉：指新加坡人造成柔通膨，只是新山少数市民看法》，1992年4月22日《联合早报》第2版）

也说"要打没好手，厮骂没好口"/"打起来没好拳，骂起来没好言"/"相骂没好口，相打没好手"。

No Nice Words When Cursing , No Nice Punch When Hitting

This old saying figuratively describes how when one is in a heated row or a brawl, reasoning and self-restraint is hardly possible.

Example: "Mr Liu, the General Manager of a travel agency, when commenting on the reported issues, says that Singapore and Malaysia being in the same family should not have quarrelled over technicalities. As there are 'no nice words when cursing and no nice punch when hitting', both parties should allow themselves to cool off." (Lianhe Zaobao 22/4/92)

依样画葫芦　yī yàng huà húlu

　　照着葫芦的样子画葫芦。比喻照着现成的样子模仿，没有创新。例如：耶尔辛要求所有的独联共和国继续采用由俄罗斯银行印刷和控制的卢布——这已是一种将近无效的货币。他还恫言，如果乌克兰发行新货币，俄罗斯也会依样画葫芦。（《乌克兰恫言要脱离独联》，1992年1月21日《联合早报》封面版）这个例句中的"依样画葫芦"相当于"照办"。

　　"依样"也说"依本"；"画"字也可以省去，说成"依样葫芦"。这条俗语也说成"依葫芦画瓢"；瓢：piáo，舀（yǎo）水或撮取面粉的器具，多半是用对半剖开的匏瓜（páoguā，比葫芦大）做的。

To Copy Exactly

　　"Hulu" is a bottle gourd. To draw hulu exactly as others have done means to copy mechanically.

　　Example: "Yeltsin asked all republics in the Commonwealth of Independent States to continue accepting roubles which are printed and controlled by Russia. And he warned that should Ukraine issue its own currency, Russia would 'copy exactly'." (Lianhe Zaobao 21/1/92)

一朝被蛇咬，三年怕井绳

yī zhāo bèi shé yǎo, sān nián pà jǐng shéng

比喻遭受了一次挫折以后就变得胆小怕事。例如：一朝被蛇咬，三年怕井绳。想到我（中国著名影星刘晓庆）从影以来已经惹出那么多事，不停地使我成为众矢之的，真是不想也不敢再惹什么事了。（《我为什么再写自传》，1992年5月1日《联合早报》《茶馆》版）

"一朝"也说"一年"，"三年"也说"十年"，"井绳"也说"草绳"和"绳索"。

Once Bitten By A Snake, One Shies At A Coiled Rope For The Next Three Years

The English equivalence of this Chinese folk adage is 'Once bitten, twice shy'.

Example: "Since I (the Chinese film star Liu Xiaoqing) started my career in the film industry, so many things have happened and I have been the target of all sorts of attacks. 'Once bitten by a snake, one shies at a coil rope for the next three years'. I really do not want, or dare to stir up any more trouble." (Lianhe Zaobao 1/5/92)

避风头 bì fēngtou

看见形势对自己不利而躲开。例如：一次，仓库物品被盗，杨怀定成了怀疑的对象。这时，他的儿子正巧患上A型肝炎，他想请假，又怕别人说是"避风头"，只得天天按时上班，接受旁人异样的目光。（《上海股市大亨"杨百万"》，1992年2月18日《联合早报》第21版）

也说"避避风头"。

To Stay Away From Trouble

Literally, this Chinese saying means to take shelter from the direct wind. It usually means to lie low.

Example: "When the factory had a break-in sometime ago, Yang Huaiding became a suspect. Coincidentally, his son contacted Hepatitis A and he wanted to take leave. However, he was worried that others might think he was 'staying away from trouble', so he decided to go to the office as usual." (Lianhe Zaobao 18/2/92)

打游击 dǎ yóujī

比喻从事没有固定地点的工作或活动。例如：中国大陆
"丐帮"南下，偷渡到香港行乞。由于有损香港形象，警方严
厉对付。这些行乞的非法入境者听到风声，就实行打游击，几
天便换一个行乞地点，逃避警方的截查。（《大陆跛丐
（bǒgài）到港行乞，月入四千至六千元》，1992年4月14日
《联合早报》第13版）

To Fight As A Guerrilla

This common saying means to carry out activities at different
places.

Example: "Beggars in mainland China have been slipping across
the border into Hongkong to beg. As this is damaging the image of
the British Colony, the police has taken harsh measures to deal with
the problem. Now these illegal entrants are resorting to 'fighting as
a guerrilla' by moving from place to place to avoid the police."
(Lianhe Zaobao 14/4/92)

馊主意 sōu zhǔyi

馊：饭、菜等变质而发出酸臭味。馊主意：比喻不高明的办法，也说成"馊点子"。例如：他更打个比喻说，河流出现大缺口的时候所造成的洪害很大，要救也来不及，不如先开些小缺口，疏导河水。子产这一番民主言论直听得只会出馊主意的大臣连声说："小人实不才"。（《何谓"好的政府"？》，1991年10月27日《联合早报》第2版）

Rotten Idea

"Sou" means stale. It is used to describe food which has gone bad.

Example: "Zi Chan, a brilliant Chinese official used an analogy to show the correct ways of solving problems. He said that it would be disastrous to open the flood-gate in order to drain a flooded river, but it could be made more manageable by opening smaller holes to allow the water to flow out slowly. His colleagues, who could only offer 'rotten ideas', admitted their ignorance." (Lianhe Zaobao 27/10/91)

无底洞　wúdǐdòng

　　永远填不满的洞。比喻没完没了的要求或永远不能满足的要求。例如：苏联曾是世界上第二个超级大国，现在竟然成为西方国家的一个累赘（léizhui）和负担，德国想方设法动员世界各国来援助这个"无底洞"。（《人们又开始怀念戈尔巴乔夫》，1992年1月29日《联合早报》第15版）

A Bottomless Pit

　　It is used to describe a demand or an appetite that can never be satisfied.

　　Example: "The Soviet Union is the world's second largest superpower, but it has now become a burden to the West, yet Germany is still trying hard to mobilise the world community to fill this 'bottomless pit'." (Lianhe Zaobao 29/1/92)

下马威 xiàmǎ wēi

从前，中国的官吏初到任，就故意用严刑峻法来处分下属，借以显示自己的威严，叫"下马威"。现指一开头就向对方显示一点厉害。例如：梅杰访问北京时，正当中国人大常委会开会，可是这次会议并没有把"国际防止核扩散条约"列入议程。这种作法，显然是中国当局的精心安排。目的是要给梅杰一个下马威。（《从梅杰访华，看中国与西方国家关系》，1991年9月4日《联合早报》第12版）

这条惯用语原本说成"下马威"或"下车作威"。

To Deal Someone A Head-on Blow At The First Encounter

In ancient time, some Chinese government officials purposely punished someone severely to show their authority on assuming duty, or at the moment they dismounted from the horse. It now comes to mean showing someone some colours.

Example: "During PM Major's visit, the Chinese government intentionally ommitted the discussion of the International Treaty on Anti Proliferation of Nuclear Weapons at the meeting of its law-making body. Apparently, it was done deliberately 'to deal Major a head-on blow at the first enounter'." (Lianhe Zaobao 4/9/91)

小九九　xiǎojiǔjiǔ

吴方言（以上海话为代表）词语，指乘法口诀。比喻算计、计划。例如：数万人来是来了，干什么呢？怎么能留得住呢？在家时一般心中都有个小九九，可一是情况了解不够，二是思想准备不足，三是情势在不断变化。因此，一进匈牙利国门，多有脸色为之变者，至于在这里发财立命、融进社会主流，则更是梦中之事了。（在《匈牙利闯天下的中国人》，1991年12月20日《联合早报》第19版）

To Have One's Own Plan

This Chinese idiom is a dialectal term originating from a pithy formula which is often in rhyme. It infers that someone already has an idea in his mind.

Example: "Thousands of people have migrated here. Can they survive? At home, at least they 'have their own plans', but now they are in a strange land with a rapidly changing environment. If they hope to get rich in Hungary, then they must be dreaming." (Lianhe Zaobao 20/12/91)

一条龙 yītiáolóng

比喻生产程序或工作环节上的紧密联系和配合。例如：关于我国商家希望海南省建立类似我国经济发展局的"一条龙"投资审批手续，减少形式主义与官僚主义，海南省省长刘剑锋说："现在比以前有很大的改善。"（《中国中央还在考虑胜宝旺集团与海南联营航线》，1992年3月28日《联合早报》封面版）

A Single Dragon

This Chinese idiom represents one continuous line, a connected sequence or a coordinated process.

Example: "Referring to the hope expressed by Singapore businessmen that Hainan could establish 'a single dragon' system similar to that of Singapore's EDB to process the proposed investment projects so as to reduce formalities and red tape, Mr Liu Jianfeng, provincial Governor of Hainan said that the process had already been greatly improved." (Lianhe Zaobao 28/3/92)

一窝蜂　yīwōfēng

形容许多人为一件事一哄而行动起来。例如：一些人唯利是图的作风，往往会把原本用意良好的措施搞坏。政府允许R片放映的目的，绝不是要让色情暴力片泛滥，但影片商马上一窝蜂的推出低级色情电影，却立刻产生了这样的效果。我们必须从中吸取教训。（《不完全是R片的问题》，1991年9月10日《联合早报》社论）

这条惯用语，也可以形容乱糟糟的局面或景象。

Like A Swarm Of Bees

This Chinese idiom figuratively describes the sudden rush of people in response to a new attraction.

Example: "The profit-mindedness of certain people often foul up a well-intentioned measure. When the government introduced R-rated films, cinema operators immediately rushed 'like a swarm of bees' to screen inferior sex and violent pictures, thus producing various undesirable effects. We must learn a lesson from this." (Lianhe Zaobao 10/9/91)

硬碰硬　yìng pèng yìng

　　有两个意思：（1）用强硬的态度对待强硬的态度，或用强力对付强力；（2）比喻不能马虎对待的工作。例如：如果贝克访问北京的时候，像美国的一些传媒所鼓吹的那样"硬碰硬"，在人权、核武扩散等问题上施压的话，中共肯定不会让步，因为现在中国的处境，与一年前已经不同了。（《北京不会向美国压力屈服》，1991年11月15日《联合早报》第19版）这个例子里的"硬碰硬"用的是第一个意思。

Confront The Tough With Toughness

　　This Chinese term has double meanings: 1) to use tough measures to deal with a tough situation or person; 2) a job that demands painstaking work or real skills.

　　Example: "While visiting China, US Secretary of State, James Baker might decide to 'confront the tough with toughness' on human rights and anti-nuclear proliferation issues as suggested by the American media. If that is so, he is unlikely to get concession from Beijing. After all, the situation in China has changed much since a year ago." (Lianhe Zaobao 15/11/91)

应声虫 yìngshēngchóng

随声而应的虫。比喻没有主见，别人怎么说就跟着怎么说的人。例如：如今苏联国将不国，各加盟共和国宣告独立，中央政府权限不明，苏联外交全无方向可言。人民甚至产生了苏联在国际政治舞台上完全成了美国应声虫的印象。（《戈谢重结盟，苏联求生存》，1991年11月21日《联合早报》社论）

A Yesman

Literally, this Chinese term describes insects which echo mindlessly with each other. It is used figuratively to describe a person who mimics others and has no opinion of his own.

Example: "Now that the Soviet Union is disintegrating, with various republics proclaiming independence, the authority of the central government is unclear and its diplomatic policy has hardly any direction to talk about. In fact, some people seem to think that in the international political area, the country has become 'a yesman' of the United States." (Lianhe Zaobao 21/11/91)

重头戏 zhòngtóuxì

北京话词语，原指京剧中唱工和做工都很繁重的戏。比喻
艰难而重要的工作。例如：如何援助苏联、帮助苏联摆脱目前
的政经困局，从而建立民主政治体制和自由市场经济，是这次
伦敦七国峰会的重头戏，也是西方七大工业国领袖与苏联总统
戈尔巴乔夫会谈的主要内容。（《伦敦峰会的划时代意义》，
1991年7月23日《联合早报》第12版）。

A Heavy Responsibility

This Chinese term is originally a Beijing dialect which refers to
the important role of an opera performer who has to sing and act at
the same time.

Example: "Helping the Soviet Union extricate itself from its
current economic predicament is 'a heavy responsibility' of the G7
meeting. It is also the main subject of discussion between leaders of
the western industrialised nations and President Gorbachev."
(Lianhe Zaobao 23/7/91)

老王卖瓜 Lǎowáng mài guā

这条歇后语的语底（后段）"自卖自夸"省略了。比喻自我夸耀、称赞或吹嘘。例如：陈之财说："结了婚，有了孩子，性格基本上已经定下来了。别人可能会觉得我比较有成熟男性的魅力。"说完，好像觉得自己有点老王卖瓜，哈哈地笑起来。（《荧光幕外，新广男艺人谁魅力无法挡？》，1991年12月8日《联合早报》《影艺焦点》版）

"老王"也说"老汉、"老头儿"或"王婆"。

To Praise One's Own Achievements

This is the first part of a two-part Chinese allegorical saying which literally refers to Old Wang who sells melons, and praises the superiority of his own goods. It is commonly used as a sarcarsm.

Example: "Chen Zhicai said that after getting married and having a child, his temperament has become more steady. Others may now feel that he has the attractiveness of a mature man. After saying this, he laughed aloud as he realised that he might be 'praising his own achievements'." (Lianhe Zaobao 8/12/91)

骑着毛驴看唱本——走着瞧
qí zhe máolǘ kàn chàngběn — zǒu zhe qiáo

唱本：曲艺或戏曲唱词的小册子。比喻事情没定下来，还在发展的过程中，须等着看结果。例如：以江泽民为核心的中共第三代领导层仍然带有浓烈的临时过渡色彩。到了中共十四大时，究竟会产生怎样的最高领导层，还是骑毛驴看唱本走着瞧。（《中共高层人事安排再度搁置》，1991年12月3日《联合早报》第12版）

"骑着毛驴"也说成"骑驴"。

Will Have To Wait And See

Literally, this Chinese saying means "reading the song scripts while riding on a donkey's back". It means things are still in progress and the outcome has yet to be determined.

Example: "The third generation leadership led by Jiang Zemin is still very much a transitional arrangement. We 'will have to wait and see' what happens when the Chinese Communist Party holds its 14th plenum later." (Lianhe Zaobao 3/12/91)

热脸贴冷屁股　rè liǎn tiē lěng pìgu

　　形容没有骨气，故意奉承、讨好或巴结别人的样子。例如：《玫瑰之夜》的制作人、方芳芳的恩师俞凯尔为爱将的遭遇叫屈。他觉得方芳芳的一片好意，完全被叶倩文的一句话否定了，让她颇有热脸贴冷屁股的无趣感。（《方芳芳热脸贴冷屁股》，1992年1月15日《联合早报》《影艺》版）

　　也说成"热脸孔贴人家冷屁股"。

To Place One's Hot Face On Someone's Cold Buttock

　　This Chinese proverb is a sarcasm deriding one who flatters others in an ignominious manner.

　　Example: "The producer of the TV serial, 'Night Of The Roses' felt sorry for the compere, Fang Fangfang who had been chided by Sally Yeh, making her feel as though she had 'placed her hot face on someone's cold buttock'." (Lianhe Zaobao 15/1/92)

秀才造反，三年不成 xiùcái zàofǎn, sān nián bù chéng

秀才：泛指读书人。只会读书的知识分子，胆小怕事，又没有武力和实力，想造反也不会成功。例如：农民本来就是中国历史上改朝换代的主要发动者。知识分子造反的实例绝无仅有，因为"秀才造反，三年不成"。（《从国情看中国的改革》，1992年1月8日《联合早报》第21版。绝无仅有：jué wú jǐn yǒu，成语，形容极其少有。）

这条歇后语也用来讽刺读书人只会读书不会做事。

A Revolt By Scholars Could Never Succeed

"Xiucai" refers to scholars in ancient China who passed the imperial exam. It also refers to those who are educated yet do not possess the physical strength to rebel against the authority.

Example: "Throughout Chinese history, farmers were inevitably the main initiators behind the downfall of one dynasty after another. There was rarely a revolt launched by the intelligentsia. As the saying goes, 'a revolt by scholars could never succeed'." (Lianhe Zaobao 8/1/92)

一锤子买卖 yī chuízi mǎimai

有条歇后语叫"沙锅里捣蒜"，一下子就把沙锅砸碎了。比喻不管成功还是不成功，蛮干一场。

"一锤子买卖"原指只做一次生意（多指因为货品价格贵，品质差，顾客不愿再来）。现多指仅仅进行一次就算了的活动。例如：刘晓庆说了一句话，给我留下深刻的印象。她说"不做一锤子买卖"。（《刘晓庆不是印象中的刘晓庆》，1992年3月15日《联合早报》《影艺焦点》版）

One-Shot Deal

This is the second part (always unstated) of a Chinese two-part allegorical saying. The descriptive first part is 'to smash garlic in a earthenware pot'. It means 'to act rashly, regardless of consequences, and end up with one-shot deals'.

Example: "Liu Xiaoqing (a Chinese film star) really impressed me when she said she would never do an 'one-shot deal' business." (Lianhe Zaobao 15/3/92)